# MUSIC
# A.D. 450–1995

BY MARK AMMONS, D.M.A.



ISBN 1–58037–053–5

Printing No. CD–1890

Mark Twain Media, Inc., Publishers
Distributed by Carson-Dellosa Publishing Company, Inc.

# TABLE OF CONTENTS

# INTRODUCTION

To understand why things happen today, we should look to the past. In order for art to develop, it had to build on the past. In order for scientific developments to occur, today's scientists must build on yesterday's dreams and unfulfilled ideas. So, too, the music of today may be viewed as the direct descendant of the music of the past.

Our music may be fully understood only when we understand our forefathers' music. This is the aim of this book. Through reading each chapter and becoming involved in the activities that follow, students will become better acquainted with their ancestors' music and understand more about their own music as well.

So, get ready for an enlightening voyage in music through the ages.

—The Author—

# TIME LINE
## A.D. 313–1995

A time line helps us understand the order in which events occur. It also helps us keep historical events in sequence. The following time line illustrates the sequence of events that affect the history of music.

313 Constantine I declares Christianity the church of state for the Roman Empire.
500 Boethius (480–524) writes *De institutione musica.*
590 Election of Pope Gregory the Great.
600s Chant collected into specific grouping. Named Gregorian chants.
650 Rise of monasteries.
800 Cultivation of music in the monasteries.
900 Arabic musical instruments introduced into Europe.
1025 Guido of Arezzo's first writings on music.
1054 Final separation of Eastern and Western churches.
1094 St. Mark's Cathedral, Venice, completed (begun 976).
1096 First crusade.
1150 Troubadours and trouvères flourish.
Notre Dame School assumes musical leadership.
1175 Leonin, master of Notre Dame School.
1183 Perotin active at Notre Dame.
1240 The motet becomes important type of polyphonic composition.
1250 Period of *Ars antiqua.*
1270 English musicians in Paris.
1300 Beginning of French *Ars nova.*
1316 Philippe de Vitry (1291–1361), *Ars nova.*
1330 Italian *Ars nova.*
1337 Outbreak of the Hundred Years' War.
1360 Guillaume de Machaut, *Notre Dame Mass.*
1440 Josquin des Prez born.
1453 End of Hundred Years' War.
1454 Gutenberg invents printing from movable metal type.
1500 Ottaviano dei Petrucci, first to print complete song collections from movable type.
1517 Martin Luther's Protestant Reformation.
1525 Giovanni Pierluigi da Palestrina born.
1531 Establishment of the Church of England.
1545 Council of Trent, reform of music in Catholic church.
1553 Giovanni Gabrieli born.
1554 Giovanni Palestrina, first book of masses.
1569 Palestrina, first book of motets.
1587 Claudio Monteverdi, first book of madrigals.
1600 Facopo Peri, *Euridice* (musical drama).

1607 Monteverdi, *Orfeo.*
First Opera.
1669 Paris Academy of Music founded.
1704 Handel, *St. John Passion.*
Georg Telemann (1681–1761) founds Collegium musicum at Leipzig.
1712 Antonio Vivaldi (1678–1741), Concertos, Op. 3.
Handel settles in London.
1715 First *opéra comique* founded.
1722 Bach, *The Well-Tempered Clavier, I.*
Rameau, *Treatise of Harmony.*
1726 Vivaldi, *The Four Seasons.*
Rameau, *New system of music theory.*
1732 Franz Joseph Haydn born.
1733 Giovanni Pergolesi (1710–1736), *La Serva padrona.*
1756 Wolfgang Amadeus Mozart born.
1762 Gluck, *Orfeo ed Euridice* (opera).
1770 Ludwig van Beethoven born.
1789 French Revolution (till 1794).
George Washington first president of the United States.
1790 Mozart, *Così fan tutte* (opera).
Haydn in London.
1791 Mozart, *The Magic Flute* (opera), *Requiem.*
Haydn, first *London* Symphonies.
1792 Ludwig van Beethoven at Vienna.
1795 Paris Conservatory founded.
1797 Franz Schubert, born.
1799 Beethoven, First Symphony, *Sonata Pathétique.*
1800 Haydn, *The Seasons.*
Discovery of ultraviolet rays.
1802 Beethoven, Second Symphony.
Napoleon made consul for life.
1811 Franz Schubert, first *Lieder.*
Franz Liszt born.
1813 Richard Wagner born.
1815 Invention of the metronome.
1821 Carl Maria von Weber (1786–1826), *Der Freischütz* (opera).
1830 First railroad, Liverpool to Manchester.
1845 Liszt, *Les Préludes.*
1851 Wagner, *Opera and Drama* (book).
1862 Claude Debussy born.
1868 Scott Joplin born.
1869 First American transcontinental railroad.
1870 Wagner, *Die Walküre* performed (music drama).
1872 Georges Bizet (1838–1875), *L'Arlésienne* (opera).

1873 W.C. Handy born.
1874 Arnold Schönberg born.
1876 First Wagner festival at Bayreuth.
1879 Edison invents an improved incandescent electrical light.
1883 Metropolitan Opera opened.
Anton von Webern born.
1894 Debussy, *Prélude à l'après-midi d'un faune* (Impressionism).
1897 John Philip Sousa (1845–1932), "The Stars and Stripes Forever."
1899 Scott Joplin, "Maple Leaf Rag."
1900 Louis Armstrong born.
1910 Igor Stravinsky (1882–1971), *The Firebird* (ballet).
1912 Schönberg, *Pierrot Lunaire* (Expressionism).
1913 Anton Webern (1883–1945), *Six Orchestral Pieces.*
Stravinsky, *Sacré du Printemps.*
1914 W.C. Handy (1873–1958), "St. Louis Blues."
1917 First recording of Dixieland Jazz.
1922 Schönberg, method of composing with twelve tones.
1924 George Gershwin (1898–1937), "Rhapsody in Blue."
1925 Alban Berg (1885–1935), *Wozzeck.*
1935 Swing (jazz) music becomes popular.
1940s Bebop (jazz) style popular.
1954 Bill Hayley and His Comets, "Rock Around the Clock," advent of rock and roll.
1955 Elvis Presley makes first record.
1964 The Beatles come to America.

# MUSIC IN THE MIDDLE AGES (A.D. 450–1450)

A medieval church choir

The period of history known as the Middle Ages began around the year A.D. 450 with the decline of the Roman Empire and spans 1000 years to around A.D. 1450. This was a time in history marked by barbaric wars, feudal disputes, and religious crusades. It was also a period of great faith. Christianity had been adopted by the Roman Empire as the church of state, and therefore, it had also been adopted by many of the countries in Europe as the major religion. Toward the end of the Middle Ages, there was a period of great cultural growth. Romanesque-style churches and monasteries and Gothic cathedrals were built, universities were founded, and cities and towns grew.

The Middle Ages also was a period in time when there was a sharp division among the social classes: the nobility, the clergy, and the peasantry. The peasants were very poor and were usually feudal subjects to the noble class. Peasants farmed the land for the nobles, and they raised their herds for them. They were very much like indentured servants. The nobility lived in fortified castles and lived lives of great ease. The clergy, or leaders of the church, were very influential in guiding the affairs of the nobility and the peasantry.

The church had a virtual monopoly on learning. Both peasants and nobles alike were generally illiterate. Cathedrals and monasteries were the centers of religious, educational, and musical life. All of the important musicians during the Middle Ages were priests and worked for the church. The only music education available during the Middle Ages was in church schools, and only boys were allowed to attend. One of the most important occupations in monasteries was liturgical singing, or the singing of chants for the services that were held throughout the day.

Almost all of the music from the Middle Ages was vocal music. Instruments were not allowed in churches or monasteries for the majority of the Middle Ages. Not until about 1100 were instruments used to accompany voices. Of all the instruments used, the organ was the most prominent.

## Activities:

1. Try to imagine what it would be like to be a priest in a monastery. Describe what your daily activities might be.

2. If you had written music for the Crusades, what would have been some of the things you might have included in your songs?

Name______________________________ Date______________________________

# QUESTION COUNTDOWN

1. The Middle Ages began in approximately what year and ended in approximately what year?

_______________________________________________

2. What religious faith was adopted by the Roman Empire as the church of state?

_______________________________________________

3. Churches and monasteries were built in what architectural style?

_______________________________________________

4. During the Middle Ages where would an individual have to go if he wanted to study music?

_______________________________________________

5. What were the three social classes in the Middle Ages?

_______________________________________________

6. At what point in the Middle Ages did we see a period of great cultural growth?

_______________________________________________

7. What was one of the most important occupations in monasteries?

_______________________________________________

8. What type of music constitutes almost all of the music from the Middle Ages?

_______________________________________________

9. What objects were not allowed in churches or monasteries for the majority of the Middle Ages?

_______________________________________________

10. Of all the instruments used, which one was the most prominent?

_______________________________________________

Name________________________________Date________________________________________

# CROSSWORD PUZZLE

Use the clues below to complete the puzzle. Answers to the questions can be found in the narrative.

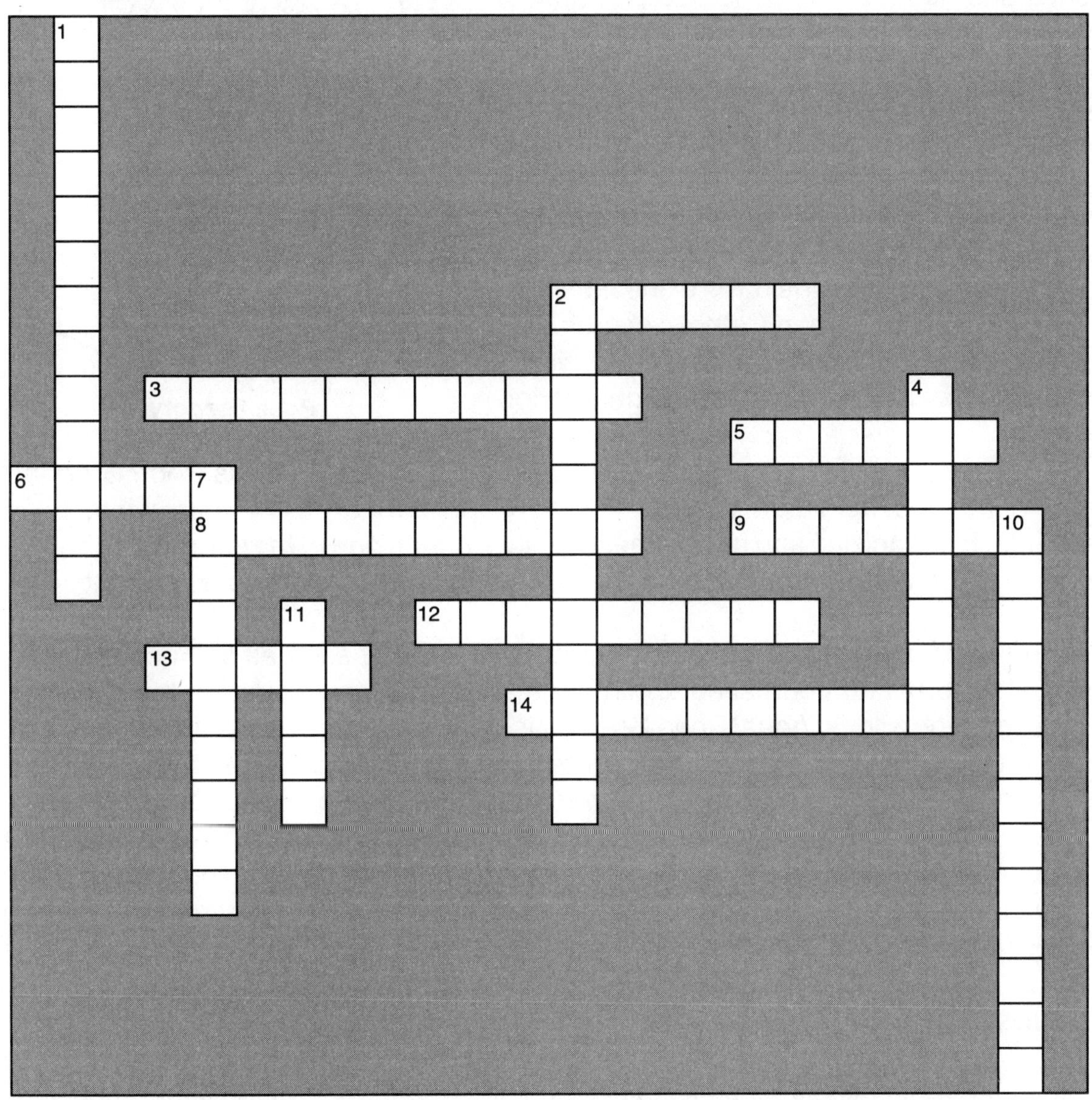

**ACROSS**

2. leaders of the church
3. Christianity was the church of state for the _____ ______.
5. lived in fortified castles
6. type of almost all music in the Middle Ages
8. unable to read and write
9. All important musicians were _______.
12. a center of religious, educational, and musical life
13. most prominent instrument in the Middle Ages
14. period of history from A.D. 450 to 1450

**DOWN**

1. only place to receive music education
2. the major religion of Europe
4. feudal subjects
7. _____ singing was an important occupation in the monasteries.
10. There was a sharp division among _____ _____ in the Middle Ages.
11. The Middle Ages was a period of great _____.

# POPE GREGORY I AND THE DOVE

Pope Gregory I

During the Middle Ages, music in the churches and monasteries consisted primarily of the singing of songs whose words were taken from the Scriptures that dealt with religious feasts or celebrations throughout the year. These feasts and celebrations constituted what is known as the liturgical year. The songs that were sung were known as *Gregorian chants.* The melodies of these songs were derived from the Greek, Hebrew, and Syrian music that formed the basis of the music for the new Christian or Roman Catholic church. For about 590 years, the melodies and their words were passed down from generation to generation orally.

In the year A.D. 590, a new pope was selected whose name was Pope Gregory the Great. He reigned from 590 to 604. During Pope Gregory's 14-year reign, he was instrumental in organizing and having these chants written down. In written form they could be taken to churches throughout Europe, and all of the same chants could be sung in every church.

The traditional myth is that Pope Gregory dictated or sang all of these melodies to a scribe after they had been sung to him by a dove that was sitting on his shoulder. In paintings from the Middle Ages, Pope Gregory is depicted sitting on his throne with a dove perched on his shoulder and whispering into his ear while a scribe takes down the words from the pope's mouth. The dove is a representation of the Spirit of God.

While this is a lovely story, in reality Pope Gregory had nothing to do with the actual writing down or transcription of the chants; however, he did have a great deal to do with their organization. These same chants have continued to be passed down in written and oral form since that time and are part of the Catholic liturgy today.

**Activities:**

1. If you had been a priest in the Catholic church in another part of the world, how do you think you would have responded to Pope Gregory's messenger when he brought the new chants to you?

2. Divide the class into two groups. Group One must argue in favor of accepting the new chants as outlined by Pope Gregory. Group Two must argue against the new chants.

3. Seat the class in a large circle. One student begins by whispering to the student next to him or her a predetermined message or story. Continue this process around the circle until the last student has heard the message. That student should repeat it aloud to the class. This will give the class an example of the oral tradition.

Name______________________________Date______________________________

# QUESTION COUNTDOWN

1. The words for the songs sung in monasteries during the Middle Ages were taken from what book(s)?

_______________________________________________

2. What types of events constituted what is known as the liturgical year?

_______________________________________________

3. From what type of music were the melodies of these songs derived?

_______________________________________________

4. What was the name of the new Christian church?

_______________________________________________

5. How long was Pope Gregory I's reign?

_______________________________________________

6. According to the traditional myth, Pope Gregory I received the chants from whom?

_______________________________________________

7. Why did Pope Gregory I have the chants written down?

_______________________________________________

_______________________________________________

8. What does the dove in the myth represent?

_______________________________________________

9. For how many years were the melodies and words passed from generation to generation in an oral tradition?

_______________________________________________

10. The new chants were to be taken to churches on what continent?

_______________________________________________

# LEONIN AND PEROTIN GO TO SCHOOL

**Example of a motet**

The Gregorian chants spoken of in the last chapter were single melodies. There was only one melody being sung to the words written. Around A.D. 1100 a very important development in music history took place. This development, known as *polyphony,* combined two or more simultaneous melodic lines. Then, instead of just one line of melody, the priests and monks in monasteries could sing two or three or four lines of melody at one time.

Having that many melodies meant that music would have to be written down in a more precise manner. In this way, the development of polyphony brought about the development of precise notation of music. The earliest known composer of polyphonic music was Leonin, who lived in the last part of the twelfth century. He was one of a number of composers whose center of study and composition was the cathedral of Notre Dame in Paris. The style of polyphony that Leonin composed was called *organum.* Organum was created by adding a second voice or second melody to the Gregorian chant. It ran parallel to that chant at the interval of a fourth, either above or below.

Leonin's successor was Perotin. Perotin wrote polyphonic music in three and four parts. Toward the end of Perotin's life composers began writing new words to be used by the additional voices. While the original Gregorian chant melody was sung with the original Gregorian chant text or words, new words would be written for the other two or three voices. The addition of these new texts resulted in what was called the *motet.* It was the most important form of early polyphonic music. The motet from the late Middle Ages could be either secular or sacred; it could have to do with a religious or nonreligious theme. (Something sacred is religious, and something secular is nonreligious.)

## Activities:

1. You are a new member of the Notre Dame School of Music. How do you feel about being a member of a group of musicians who are creating new music that has never been heard before?

2. Find a simple melody and create your own form of polyphony.

3. As a class learn a simple melody as an example of monophony, then learn a melody that can be sung in a round or a canon as a simple example of polyphony.

Name______________________________Date_____________________________________

# QUESTION COUNTDOWN

1. What is the combination of two or more simultaneous melodic lines?

2. What development did polyphony bring about?

3. Who was the earliest known composer of polyphony?

4. What was the name of the cathedral at which he and a number of other composers studied?

5. What was the style of polyphony called that Leonin composed?

6. Who was Leonin's successor?

7. Perotin wrote polyphonic music in how many parts?

8. What was the most important form of early polyphonic music?

9. What type of theme could a motet have?

10. What is the difference between sacred and secular?

Name________________________________Date________________________________

# WORD SEARCH

Find the terms listed below. They may be printed in the puzzle horizontally, vertically, diagonally, or backward. All of the words are associated with the narrative in some way.

```
I Q V M M Y D N K G O Z K I F Z L V H K
C W V E I O D H M Q K R K B G A N L L M
H D V Q D V N O D Q R W W V R O Z M Q T
X P W M D V P S L F N N E D T O U H L R
O O S L L S H Q O E U N E R Y N J H A W
Y T W U E A W T I Z M H E X A P O I Z R
K N I C A C T V A L T D I G V T B B P B
R A V U G R T Y E A A B R F Y W L A O I
A H E F E E W F C M M O D S V E R O L E
L C G W S D R A E P O M U E G L T W Y I
U N I V M L E J N T M O A C I F S M P N
C A Z Z G W S R P E V N P O T T S S H T
E I E V V H O V A T G A A N K H O R O E
S R Z Q R G P L R O N S R D Z C C H N R
V O L M F S M T A M I T I V W E P P Y V
N G E Q E X O Q L M T E S O K N B T U A
B E O B P A C K L L O R V I O T I K J L
G R N A H W R F E A R I P C L U E S W F
T G I B U Q S L L C E E L E S R Q O I H
R Z N O T A T I O N P S I H U Y J V T P
```

1. cathedral
2. composer
3. Gregorian chants
4. interval
5. Leonin
6. melody
7. Middle Ages
8. monasteries
9. motet
10. notation
11. Notre Dame
12. organum
13. parallel
14. Paris
15. Perotin
16. polyphony
17. sacred
18. second voice
19. secular
20. twelfth century

# TROUBADOURS, TROUVÈRES, AND JONGLEURS

A jongleur

The vast majority of music in the beginning of the Middle Ages was written and performed for the religious services of the Roman Catholic church. Toward the end of the Middle Ages, however, a substantial amount of secular music, or music that could be sung outside of the church, appeared. This music was performed by groups of musicians known as troubadours, trouvères, and jongleurs.

The troubadours and trouvères were active in France, the troubadours to the south and the trouvères to the north. They were medieval poet musicians that catered to the upper class, or the nobility. These musicians presented original and new material that was vastly different from the music sung in the churches of the day, and their names, *troubadour* and *trouvère,* even meant "finder" or "inventor." Poems of the troubadours and trouvères ranged from simple ballad love songs to political and moral tunes, from war songs to laments to dance songs.

Jongleurs were a class of musicians who wandered from town to town and were very versatile entertainers. Many played instruments, sang and danced, juggled, showed tricks and animal acts, and performed plays. To the common folk of the Middle Ages, the jongleurs functioned as a sort of traveling newspaper, passing on gossip and news to each new town. The jongleurs, however, were viewed as vagabonds and lived on the fringe of society.

To medieval court life, secular music was very important. It provided entertainment before, during, and after dinner—and also accompanied dancing. It was also important to the ceremonies that welcomed visiting dignitaries and helped strengthen the spirits of warriors departing on the Crusades.

**Activities:**

1. Describe what life may have been like as a jongleur.

2. Create and/or perform music that could have been used in the courts of the nobility.

3. As a class, organize and practice a "medieval concert" including period songs, juggling, and acrobatics similar to those performed by the troubadours and jongleurs.

Name______________________________ Date______________________________

# QUESTION COUNTDOWN

1. What do the terms *troubadour* and *trouvère* mean?

____________________________________________________________

2. What type of music did the troubadours and trouvères perform?

____________________________________________________________

3. The vast majority of music in the Middle Ages was written and performed for which church?

____________________________________________________________

4. What class of musicians wandered from town to town as versatile entertainers?

____________________________________________________________

5. What type of music was important to medieval court life?

____________________________________________________________

6. How did music affect the spirits of warriors departing on the Crusades?

____________________________________________________________

7. What were some of the things jongleurs did as entertainers?

____________________________________________________________

8. To the common folk of the Middle Ages, what was the function of the jongleurs?

____________________________________________________________

9. How were the jongleurs viewed in society?

____________________________________________________________

10. What were some of the different topics covered by the poems of the troubadours and trouvères?

____________________________________________________________

# "NEW ART" vs. "OLD ART"

Advancements in notation allowed for increased use of polyphonic music.

Throughout history, time periods are generally given a starting date and an ending date. These periods do not change suddenly in a specific year, however. The transition from one period of history to the next, whether it be music or art or social history, begins many years before the traditional beginning year given for each period.

The transition from the Middle Ages to the next period in music history, called the Renaissance, began in the fourteenth century, at least 100 years before the date of 1450 that historians give. An important aspect of this transition was the clash of the "new art" and the "old art", also called *ars nova* and *ars antiqua.* The "old art" was typified by music for the church. In particular, the motets and organum of Leonin and Perotin fall under this style. The "new art", or ars nova, was typified by the new-found interest in secular music, or music for occasions outside of the church. The new music that was written was polyphonic music, but it was not based on Gregorian chant. It included drinking songs and music that imitated the sounds of animals and hunters' shouts.

This new style of music was only possible due to the further development of a new notational system (a way of writing down music) by a man named Philippe de Vitry (1291–1361). Philippe de Vitry was one of the outstanding poets and composers of his time.

The vast majority of the changes in music that became known as the ars nova occurred in French and Italian music. One of the most important composers of this new music form was a Frenchman named Guillaume de Machaut (1300–1377).

## Activities:

1. Was "old art" or "new art" better music? Should the "old art" have been discarded entirely, or should the "new art" have been ignored?

2. Explore any other interesting developments outside the world of music that were occurring at this time (c. 1350–1450).

3. Look at examples of early notation, such as that developed by Philippe de Vitry, and modern notation. Experiment with writing in both styles of notation.

Name________________________________Date________________________________

# WORD SEARCH

Find the terms listed below. They may be printed in the puzzle horizontally, vertically, diagonally, or backward. All of the words are associated with the narrative in some way.

P T T S O Y K R T I X N D K W C I D C H

G P H S C N O N Q G R I I F A P I C M U

K R C I S U M R A L U C E S R H I P W W

N Q E S L K D O A T T F G O S I G W Y L

S V C T M A Z I L W Q L F C A L Y T M N

X Q Q I G S Y U K D O F H I N I C M G I

E J A R N F F R G H A S E S T P A I X Q

Y C M Y N O D A S M U R G U I P G D S A

C F N G W T H U G C L J T M Q E E D Y N

V G N A P E B P U N J C B H U D Q L Q I

X W A A S S Z V Y C R U O C A E R E A M

E D W R V S D M J L B R O R D V O A P A

H V S M S O I O K U O V J U O I P G G L

O W C Y L Q N A S W N P O H R T D E S S

B N X W Z B N S N G V Q M C G R R S Q O

H Q Q U C G C E R E V F Z N A Y C X U U

N N M N E W A R T A R G U L N J C Y E N

H B E J V W E O V S Z Y K G U G C I T D

L Q X X Z M F D G Z X U Z Q M J T H S S

L Z G U I L L A U M E D E M A C H A U T

1. new art
2. old art
3. Middle Ages
4. Renaissance
5. ars nova
6. ars antiqua
7. church music
8. organum
9. secular music
10. polyphonic
11. animal sounds
12. Philippe de Vitry
13. Guillaume de Machaut

# MUSIC IN THE RENAISSANCE (A.D. 1450–1600)

The printing press popularized the music of the great composers.

The Renaissance—or "rebirth"—actually began to occur closer to the end of the Middle Ages through society and culture in general. It is considered a time of great creativity, exploration, and adventure. The arts, the sciences, and learning became extremely important aspects of life during this time period. In the Renaissance the church lost a great deal of its power because of the Protestant Reformation led by Martin Luther. The church no longer monopolized learning. The middle and upper classes began to view learning and education as status symbols and hired people to educate their children.

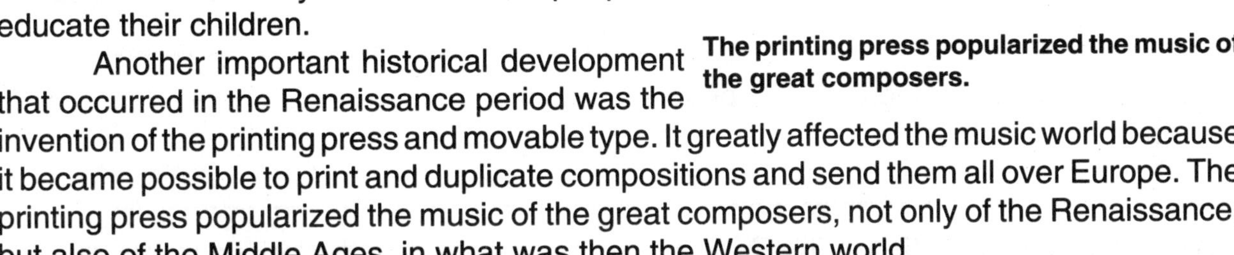

Another important historical development that occurred in the Renaissance period was the invention of the printing press and movable type. It greatly affected the music world because it became possible to print and duplicate compositions and send them all over Europe. The printing press popularized the music of the great composers, not only of the Renaissance, but also of the Middle Ages, in what was then the Western world.

Every educated person was expected to be trained in music. When education shifted from the clergy to the middle and upper classes, musical activity shifted from the churches to the courts of the nobility. The music of the Renaissance period continued to include both sacred and secular forms of music, but a greater emphasis was placed on instrumental forms of music. In general, music in the Renaissance, along with all the other arts and sciences, developed and expanded in many ways never before thought possible.

**Activities:**

1. Decide whether you want to be a poet, scientist, artist, or musician during the Renaissance period. Describe what life might have been like for you.

2. An important meeting called the Council of Trent occurred during the Renaissance. Look up the Council of Trent in an encyclopedia. How could it have affected the music world?

3. Leonardo da Vinci was an active scientist and artist during this time period. Research some of his scientific developments and ideas, and present them to the class.

Name______________________________Date______________________________

# QUESTION COUNTDOWN

1. What is another word for *Renaissance?*

_______________________________________________

2. What are some characteristics of the Renaissance period?

_______________________________________________

3. What aspects of life became more important during the Renaissance period?

_______________________________________________

4. Who led the Protestant Reformation?

_______________________________________________

5. What social classes began to hire people to educate their children?

_______________________________________________

6. What important invention in the Renaissance period greatly affected the music world?

_______________________________________________

7. What type of person was expected to be trained in music during the Renaissance?

_______________________________________________

8. Musical activity shifted from one area to another. What were the names of these areas?

_______________________________________________

9. What forms of music received greater emphasis during the Renaissance period?

_______________________________________________

10. How did the invention of the printing press affect the musical world?

_______________________________________________

_______________________________________________

# JOSQUIN: THE MAN, THE MYTH, THE GREAT

**Josquin des Prez**

Josquin des Prez was born around A.D. 1440 in France. He is typically classified as one of the greatest—if not the greatest—composers of the Renaissance period. It has been said of Josquin that he was one of the first composers to show true genius in Western music. The Protestant reformer Martin Luther said of Josquin, "He is the master of the notes. They must do as he wills; as for the other composers, they have to do as the notes will."

As a composer, Josquin des Prez showed a remarkable ability to combine the musical elements, devices, and novelties of the time period into music that would endure without being dated. The music of the late Middle Ages and early Renaissance showed signs of advance in the use of *counterpoint* (the pitting of one melody against another). Josquin showed an unusual ease in his compositions in the use of counterpoint and depth of emotion that had not been seen before in the music of the Middle Ages or Renaissance.

An extremely prolific composer, during his lifetime Josquin wrote 18 settings of the Roman Catholic mass, 6 settings of different mass sections, 112 motets (vocal pieces for three or four voices), and 70 chansons (songs with three voices, in which either one or two of the lower voices are instruments). The number of motets that he wrote is interesting because the mass was the primary sacred composition of the day. However, the motet allowed the composer to experiment more because it wasn't tied so closely to the church service. The motet, then, became the main vehicle that composers used to explore the newly developing compositional techniques of the Renaissance period. Josquin's motets and mass settings are the most ingenious of the time and show his talents well.

Josquin was the first of many great "transition" composers in music history. He helped to close off the Medieval period and launch the musical world into the Renaissance.

**Activities:**

1. Josquin was called a "transition" composer because his life spanned portions of two different musical eras. Our lives will span portions of two different centuries. How do you think you will feel at the beginning of the twenty-first century?

2. What is counterpoint? Can you think of any songs that might use counterpoint?

3. Write a "free" composition of eight to 12 measures. After you have finished, describe to the class your feelings as you composed the piece. The piece you composed would make up only a fraction of one of the pieces that Josquin wrote.

Name________________________ Date________________________

# QUESTION COUNTDOWN

1. Who is typically classified as one of the greatest composers of the Renaissance period?

______________________________________________________________

2. Who said this of Josquin: "He is the master of the notes. They must do as he wills"?

______________________________________________________________

3. Define the term *counterpoint.*

______________________________________________________________

4. How did Josquin's compositions differ from the compositions of composers who lived before him?

______________________________________________________________

5. Why was Josquin considered a prolific composer?

______________________________________________________________

6. What form of music was considered the primary sacred composition of the day?

______________________________________________________________

7. What did the motet allow the composer to do?

______________________________________________________________

8. Which of Josquin's compositions are the most ingenious of the time?

______________________________________________________________

9. Why was Josquin considered a "transition" composer?

______________________________________________________________

10. Which two periods of music history did Josquin's life span?

______________________________________________________________

# SACRED MUSIC: THE MOTET AND MASS

**Motets were often written for four voices.**

In the Middle Ages the development of the *motet* (a vocal piece for three or four voices) was used in both sacred and secular settings. In the Renaissance, the motet became a purely sacred form. Also in the Middle Ages, the motet had more than one text, often a different text for each line of melody. In the Renaissance, the motet had only one text, and it was always a Latin text. The most popular motets were usually in three or four voices. Later in the Renaissance, the motets gained additional voices, until as many as five or six voice parts could be written in a motet.

The *mass* was another extremely important form of music in the Renaissance. The mass is the most important religious service in the Roman Catholic church. It consists of two different parts. The *proper,* which had a number of different sections, would change each day. The *ordinary* had five sections, and the order of those five sections was never changed. The five sections of the ordinary of the mass were the *Kyrie, Gloria, Credo, Sanctus,* and *Agnus Dei.* The Kyrie was called a prayer for mercy; the Gloria was a joyful hymn of praise; the Credo was a confession of faith; the fourth section, the Sanctus, is the section that lauds the holiness of God; and the Agnus Dei, the last section, praises the Lamb of God who takes away the sins of the world. Most of the settings of the mass in the Renaissance period were based on a fragment of a Gregorian chant. That fragment became the basic melody upon which all of the other parts of the mass were written. There are a number of masses for special occasions, but perhaps the most important is the mass for the dead, the *Requiem,* which is sung at funerals and memorial services.

The mass and motet represent two of the most important forms of sacred music in the Renaissance. In later periods of music these forms would be further developed and embellished.

**Activities:**

1. Can you think of any songs that you know that might be similar to motets? How are they similar? How are they different? Ask your teacher to let you listen to a short motet so that you can compare them more easily.

2. If possible, take the students on a field trip to a monastery where they can experience a Catholic Mass in its entirety. As an alternative, take the students to a nearby Catholic church to observe its services.

Name_______________________________ Date_______________________________

# WORD SEARCH

Find the terms listed below. They may be printed in the puzzle horizontally, vertically, diagonally, or backward. All of the words are associated with the narrative in some way.

I X M F A X Y U F O H J B H M H C R Q G

O O O M J D X N E D M O J B Z X K U V U

E J T Q N O I S S E F N O C U O F N Y G

F F E I M N F J X R Y Q P R I R J Z Y N

Z M T D K M N R C C D J X I H A F S P M

N M Q Y W Q Y I I S W W E E K C I Y J Y

R N R I I S K C G J X P H D Y L G Y G H

E I C Q V J J G R W N K B S L A L M X L

E F M E G B Y Y D E T A J U O S F Q S U

O W U O L B W O K A M X R N C Z C H E F

H P E A I R O L G T E R S G I W T S N Y

P S J M K T F K M W E Y O A R I F I N O

V X Y E N S U T C N A S I F G B J Y P J

R Q N I H Z O Z P S S A M K R Q O R S R

B B Z U L K V N L U O B M B X E O U U X

H Y B Q R D O R D I N A R Y P P Y K Z E

U K S E B V Y F R O V N N Q E B L A L R

Q K Y R E K T L L H U B T R V U K C R D

H P T W G U V B S Y R A M N I G R I V P

W S S E N I L O H Q U R O S Y S Y S L F

1. motet
2. Virgin Mary
3. mass
4. proper
5. ordinary
6. Kyrie
7. Gloria
8. Credo
9. Sanctus
10. Agnus Dei
11. prayer for mercy
12. joyful hymn
13. confession
14. holiness
15. Requiem

# SECULAR MUSIC: RENAISSANCE "POP"

**Most educated people included music in their studies.**

A good way to think of secular music versus sacred music is to think of music that is usually sung in church services today as sacred music, and of today's "pop" music as secular music. Secular music in the Renaissance became a very important form of expression for the educated and advanced composers of the period. Three of the most important genres (types) are the *chanson,* the instrumental dance music, and the *madrigal.*

The fifteenth-century chanson was typically composed and sung in the courts of the dukes of Burgundy and the kings of France. The chansons consisted generally of three voices, with one or both of the two lower voices being played by instruments. The music was set to the love poetry of the French Renaissance. Two important composers of the Burgundian chanson were Johannes Ockeghem (1410–1497) and Roland de Lassus (1532–1594).

Instruments became very important to the Renaissance cultures. In particular, instrumental dance music became extremely popular. The dances primarily originated in the courts of the nobility and were of a stately manner. They were often similar to vocal works such as the chansons but were played rather than sung. The instruments used in these dances were not usually specified. This allowed as much versatility as possible with regard to what instruments were available. Usually, the instrumentation for the dances was determined by whether the performances were going to be indoors or outdoors. If they were indoors, indoor instruments would be used. These instruments included recorders and bowed, string instruments similar to the strings of today. Outdoor performances would call for instruments such as the *shawm* (a medieval oboe) or *sackbutt* (the medieval trombone). Percussion instrument parts were usually not written in the music but were generally improvised at the performance. Some types of dances were the *pavane,* the *saltarello,* the *galliard,* the *allemande,* and the *ronde.*

The madrigal was one of the major forms of secular music in the Renaissance. It became the motet of secular music. It was similar in construction, generally with four to six voices, and dealt with a variety of subjects such as love, unsatisfied desire, humor, satire, and politics. One of the most famous composers of the Renaissance madrigal was Claudio Monteverdi.

**Activity:**

1. Listen to some secular music from the Renaissance. How is it similar to or different from today's "pop" music?

Name____________________________Date____________________________

# QUESTION COUNTDOWN

1. What type of music today would be the equivalent of secular music in the Renaissance period?

____________________________________________________________

2. What were the three most important genres or types of Renaissance secular music?

____________________________________________________________

3. How many voices did the chansons consist of?

____________________________________________________________

4. Who were two of the important composers of the Burgundian chanson?

____________________________________________________________

5. What type of poetry constituted the text of the Burgundian chanson?

____________________________________________________________

6. What type of music was extremely popular in Renaissance culture?

____________________________________________________________

7. What was the determining factor of the instrumentation for dances?

____________________________________________________________

8. List two examples of outdoor instruments:

____________________________________________________________

9. What were the five types of dances?

____________________________________________________________

10. What is considered the "motet" of secular music?

____________________________________________________________

# PALESTRINA AND GABRIELI: THE ITALIANS ARE COMING!

Giovanni Pierluigi da Palestrina

Two of the most important composers from the country of Italy during the Renaissance were Giovanni Pierluigi da Palestrina (1525–1594) and Giovanni Gabrieli (1557–1612). These composers typified the music of the high Renaissance and were each innovators in their own right.

Palestrina responded to the call from the Catholic church to further reform the music used in the church. He wrote glorious mass settings throughout the late 1500s. He composed over 100 masses, 375 motets, and over 90 madrigals. His compositional style included the multivoiced *(polyphonic)* techniques of his predecessors that he refined to produce a texture in which all voices were perfectly balanced.

Giovanni Gabrieli was one of the many composers who bridged the Renaissance and Baroque periods. Gabrieli's most important contributions to music were his use of multiple choirs placed in different locations in the cathedrals and the use of large forces, including instruments, in his compositions. Gabrieli was the first composer to indicate dynamics in his instrumental music. He strove to take full advantage of the dynamic contrasts that were possible between string and wind groups. He was also a prolific composer who wrote 94 motets, 7 mass movements, 30 madrigals, and over 100 instrumental solo and ensemble pieces.

The work of these two great composers helped to establish the foundations in music upon which the composers of the Baroque period would build their musical world.

**Activities:**

1. Name some important events that were happening in the world at the time of Palestrina and Gabrieli. You may have to look in an encyclopedia or history book to find some interesting answers.

2. Sing a round Gabrieli-style. Gather into three groups that are fairly even. Each group should go to a separate place in the classroom before beginning the round. Sing a song that most of you will be familiar with, such as "Row, Row, Row Your Boat" or "Frere Jacques." Individually, go and stand in the middle of the classroom to listen. While listening in the middle, does the music sound different to you when you sing in the separate groups rather than when everyone sings in one, big group?

Name________________________________Date________________________________

# CROSSWORD PUZZLE

Use the clues below to complete the crossword puzzle. Answers to the clues can be found in the narrative.

**ACROSS**

3. The country that these composers came from.
4. Palestrina wrote 375 of these.
6. The period after the Renaissance.
10. The Catholic church called for this, with regard to music.
13. He wrote glorious mass settings.
15. Together, Palestrina and Gabrieli composed over 120 of these.
17. What a piece of music a composer writes is called.
18. These composers typified the music of the ____ Renaissance.
19. Gabrieli employed the use of large ______ in his compositions.

**DOWN**

1. The first composer to indicate dynamics.
2. What a group of singers is called.
4. Gabrieli wrote seven of these.
5. The location where choirs sang.
7. Multivoiced.
8. Palestrina's middle name.
9. Palestrina's and Gabrieli's first name.
11. Not one choir, but . . . _____ _____. (two words)
12. Two groups of instruments that Gabrieli contrasted.
14. The period after the Middle Ages.
16. It tells you to play or sing softly or loudly.

# MUSIC IN THE BAROQUE PERIOD (1600–1750)

An early eighteenth-century orchestra

The Renaissance period ushered in the rebirth and rediscovery of the arts such as music, painting, sculpture, and poetry and also saw the beginning of some scientific discoveries. The Baroque period saw a refinement of science and further advances in that field. These advances helped to pave the way for new inventions and, gradually, the improvement of medicine, mining, navigation, and industry.

Music history in the Baroque period has many fine composers. Four of the best-known composers of the Baroque period are George Frideric Handel, Johann Sebastian Bach, Antonio Vivaldi, and Claudio Monteverdi. The music written by these composers was written largely on commission, meaning that the composers were asked to write a certain piece for a specific occasion. The courts of the aristocracy, churches, opera houses, and municipalities commissioned music. They employed musicians and required new music for each occasion. Composers of this period tended to use a more *homophonic* texture in their music (one main melody accompanied by either other voices or instruments) in contrast to the polyphonic style of the Renaissance age. They stressed the contrasts of sound, such as solo singers against a chorus or voices against instruments.

Music in the Baroque period also had several distinct characteristics. *Unity of mood* meant that a Baroque piece usually expressed one basic emotion. Rhythmic patterns that were heard at the beginning of the piece and repeated throughout were referred to as *unity of rhythm*. An opening melody that was heard again and again in the course of a piece was called *continuity of melody*. *Terraced dynamics* meant that the volume tended to stay constant for a period of time, and that when the dynamics did shift, it was sudden, as if stepping from one dynamic level to another. Gradual changes in dynamics were <u>not</u> typical of Baroque music. The words and meanings of the words were depicted vividly in the music. This was called *word painting*. For example, the word *heaven* might be set to a high tone or to notes moving upward and the word *hell* to a lower tone or a descending scale.

Also in the Baroque period, there were two very important developments in the use of musical groups. One was the beginning of the orchestra. The orchestra evolved into a performing group that was based on instruments from the violin family. Certain woodwind and brass instruments were added as the Baroque period progressed. The other new form was opera. Up to the beginning of the Baroque period, opera hadn't existed. At the very beginning of the Baroque period, opera developed as an important art form. Perhaps the most important composer to help develop opera was the great composer Claudio Monteverdi.

**Activity:**

1. Find a short poem. How would you compose a piece of music to fit this poem that would use the principles of word painting?

Name________________________________Date________________________________

# QUESTION COUNTDOWN

1. List two of the fine composers of the Baroque period.

_______________________________________________

2. When a composer wrote a piece of music for a certain occasion, what was that called?

_______________________________________________

3. Who typically commissioned music?

_______________________________________________

4. Define *homophonic* texture.

_______________________________________________

5. What contrasts of sound did composers stress?

_______________________________________________

6. When a piece of music expresses one basic emotion, what is it called?

_______________________________________________

7. What is unity of rhythm?

_______________________________________________

8. What is continuity of melody?

_______________________________________________

9. What are terraced dynamics?

_______________________________________________

10. What are the two important developments in the use of musical groups during the Baroque period?

_______________________________________________

Name______________________________ Date______________________________

# CROSSWORD PUZZLE

Use the clues below to complete the puzzle. Answers to the questions can be found in the narrative.

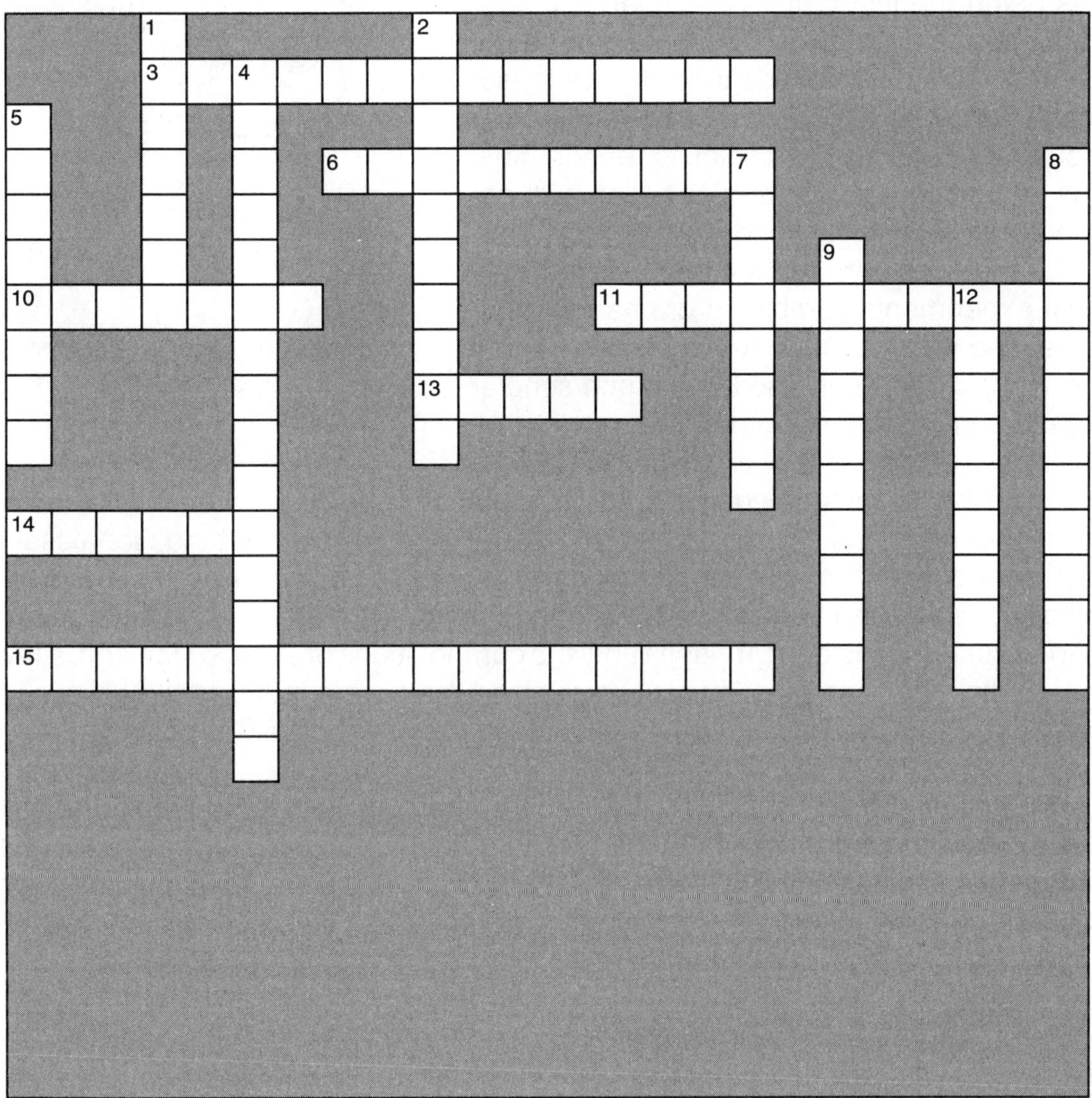

**ACROSS**

3. _____ _____ was a well-known composer of the Baroque period.
6. one main melody accompanied by either instruments or other voices
10. In the Baroque period there was a refinement of ______ .
11. expresses one basic emotion
13. new musical form of the Baroque period
14. The orchestra was based on instruments from the ______ family.
15. great composer who helped to develop opera

**DOWN**

1. George Frideric Handel was a composer of the ______ period.
2. Most composers wrote music on _____ .
4. sudden shifts in volume after long periods of staying constant
5. New music was required for each _____.
7. Baroque composers stressed the _____ of sound.
8. depicting words and meanings vividly in music
9. ______ of melody meant an opening melody was heard again and again throughout the piece.
12. new musical group developed in the Baroque period

# CLAUDIO MONTEVERDI: OPERA IS COOL!

**Claudio Monteverdi**

Claudio Monteverdi (1567–1643) is credited as being the first major composer of opera. Indeed, his opera *Orfeo* (1607) is viewed as the first modern opera. Simply defined, an opera is a drama that is sung. It combines several different elements of music such as soloists, ensembles, chorus, orchestra, and sometimes ballet, with poetry and drama, acting, scenery, and costumes.

In the sixteenth century there were many musical experiments combining drama with music. The idea was not new. A story that was told through music had been used in a much simpler fashion in ancient Greek culture. The new name that was given to this style was called *monody*—a single vocal line accompanied by a few inconspicuous chords. However, with the tremendous musical developments that had been taking place throughout the Renaissance and toward the beginning of the Baroque period, a simple melody accompanied by a few inconspicuous chords could not hold the attention nor the interest of either the composer, the performer, or the listener. It wasn't until the compositions of Jacopo Peri and, a few years later, Claudio Monteverdi that musicians realized there were many exciting ways in which this newly rediscovered style of monody could be used effectively to portray the drama of opera.

In Monteverdi's opera *Orfeo* there are numerous *arias* (solo pieces for a singer), chorus pieces, and orchestral preludes and interludes. Monteverdi's treatment of each of these types or aspects of the opera is what helped launch opera as a new and exciting art form.

**Activities:**

1. With a group or as a class, find a play that sounds interesting. Choose a part, and sing your lines. Opera is similar to this.

2. Listen to a recording of one or two of the arias from Monteverdi's opera *Orfeo*. What do you think of this piece? Can you think of any ways that it is similar to other music that you have heard? Do you think Monteverdi's music might have had any influence on the music that you listen to today?

3. If possible, as a class, go to a live performance of an opera. As an alternative, watch a video recording of an oepra, perferably an early Baroque opera such as *Orfeo*.

Name______________________________ Date______________________________

# WORD SEARCH

Find the terms listed below. They may be printed in the puzzle horizontally, vertically, diagonally, or backward. All of the words are associated with the narrative in some way.

```
N Z U O I T T R D W X X J B A E J U D D
K U U P Z C D H N R E V S A L S R E E L
T D O E N N G G J B A D P A G P W K X S
K R B R M L Y E A A C M W S U D F S P S
U T C A P T R U C H H D A C N B E F E O
L E F T Y B E M O N O D Y C S L M C R L
X A V E J A N J P Z R J O P B I E X I O
Y M K L K R E K O O U X F M Z R Q B M I
C O O L V L C T O S S G E L D E D A E S
O N R A H C S N R P O S A M W P G M N T
S T X B A I R A C F N C S X S V Z K T S
T E F O R F E O H E G M P D U W S L S X
U V P P L N Z V E O F C I Y K I U K S C
M E H J Y G A V S H O I D U A L C T T X
E R V E C S V K T L M A R X E B O Z H N
S D F B L G C S R L J I J N Q R U Q I C
K I Q H O X Y E A J B W Q H Y I T X E M
C H Q Y J E U Q O R A B U O C Z P P U E
F E U N C T O Q G R E E K C U L T U R E
H I A C L Y G I N M A T I N A X G P R T
```

1. Claudio
2. Monteverdi
3. Orfeo
4. opera
5. drama
6. soloists
7. ensembles
8. chorus
9. orchestra
10. scenery
11. experiments
12. monody
13. Peri
14. aria
15. Jacopo
16. Greek culture
17. story
18. Baroque
19. costumes
20. ballet

# INSTRUMENTS CAN MAKE BEAUTIFUL MUSIC, TOO!

**Solo instruments: harpsichord, violin, trumpet, and oboe**

Throughout the Renaissance period, an ongoing development of instrumental music as a valid and useful art form can be seen. Instruments began to find their way into more and more types of music. Toward the end of the Renaissance, instrumental music began to find its way into church music as well, at first as accompaniment. In the Baroque period, instrumental music became one of the main forms of music and of composition. The orchestra became an extremely important musical entity. It was used for accompaniment in operas and later in sacred choral music. It also came to be seen as a group that performed music written specifically for the orchestra.

The organ, through the playing of virtuosi (highly skilled musicians) such as Johann Sebastian Bach, became an important instrument in the Baroque music repertoire. Most solo music, particularly the early Baroque, was written for keyboard instruments such as the harpsichord, clavichord, and organ. Later in the Baroque period other instruments such as the violin, the oboe, and the trumpet received solo treatment. Listed below are some of the important instrumental forms of the Baroque period.

•The *chamber sonata* was written and designed to be played outside of the church, generally in a small parlor setting in a person's home. It usually had one to six or eight instruments—often string instruments—accompanied by keyboard.

•The *church sonata* was similar in instrumentation to the chamber sonata, but was designed primarily for performance in the church. The church sonata had a more serious tone and did not use the popular dance rhythms of the chamber sonata.

•*French and Italian overtures* were used as overtures, or preludes, to operas and sacred choral works, such as the *oratorio* (a type of sacred opera). The French overture generally began with a slow section and moved to a faster section, while the Italian overture consisted of three sections: fast, slow, and fast.

•*The Baroque suite* was a series of dance movements all in the same key. Unlike the dance music of the Renaissance period, however, the Baroque suite was generally used or performed in concert settings rather than in social settings where people might dance.

**Activities:**

1. Imagine that you are living during the Baroque period and are attending a church where a small ensemble of instruments is performing during the service. Suddenly, the ensemble begins performing a chamber sonata, with some very lively dance rhythms, instead of a church sonata. How do you think that you and those around you would have responded?

2. Listen to examples of each instrumental form of music: the chamber sonata, the church sonata, the overture, and the Baroque suite. How are they alike? How are they different?

Name______________________________ Date______________________________

# MATCHING

Match the term in Column A with its definition in Column B. Place the letter of the correct definition on the line next to the corresponding term in Column A.

| Column A | Column B |
|---|---|
| _____ 1. Baroque suite | a. Serious, did not use dance rhythms |
| _____ 2. French overture | b. How instrumental music was first used in church music |
| _____ 3. Italian overture | c. Virtuoso organist |
| _____ 4. church sonata | d. Useful art form |
| _____ 5. chamber sonata | e. An early Baroque keyboard instrument |
| _____ 6. Johann Sebastian Bach | f. Type of sacred opera |
| _____ 7. keyboard instruments | g. Period when instrumental music became a main form of music and composition |
| _____ 8. violin, oboe, and trumpet | h. One to eight instruments |
| _____ 9. orchestra | i. Period of development for instrumental music |
| _____ 10. instrumental music | j. Slow-fast pattern |
| _____ 11. oratorio | k. Accompanied opera and sacred choral music |
| _____ 12. organ | l. Fast-slow-fast pattern |
| _____ 13. Baroque period | m. Harpsichord and clavichord |
| _____ 14. accompaniment | n. Other instruments to receive solo treatment |
| _____ 15. Renaissance period | o. Dance movements all in the same key |

# BACH AND HANDEL: PUTTING IT TOGETHER

**Johann Sebastian Bach (left) and George Frideric Handel (right)**

Two of history's greatest composers came from the Baroque period: Johann Sebastian Bach and George Frideric Handel. These two great composers epitomized the music of the Baroque period. Drawing on all of the tools and developments in music up to their time, they developed two of the most important musical forms still used today: the *oratorio* and the *cantata.*

J.S. Bach (1685–1750) was born in Eisenach, Germany, to a family of musicians who had supplied musicians to churches and town bands in that area for a century and a half. Early in his career it was evident that he was destined for greatness. He became one of the first great organ *virtuosi* (the plural of a performer who has great technical ability on an instrument). During his lifetime, he would be invited to cities throughout Europe to both perform on and try out new organs in churches.

The cantata is a work for vocalists, chorus, and instrumentalists based on a poetic narrative of a dramatic nature. While cantatas may be based on either secular or sacred themes, all of Bach's cantatas were on sacred themes. The difference between a cantata and an opera is that the cantata is not dramatized. There is no action put to the musical words. It is generally to be performed in a church service. Bach's cantatas generally had anywhere from five to eight movements that could be made up of solo arias, choruses, or a combination of the two.

George Frideric Handel (1685–1759) was born in Halle, Germany. He was a violinist by trade. He wrote numerous operas, orchestral works, and chamber pieces, as well as keyboard music and secular vocal music, but he was best known for his twelve oratorios.

An oratorio is a large-scale musical work for solo voices, chorus, and orchestra, and it is based, as a rule, on a story from the Bible. The first oratorios were sacred operas and were produced as operas, complete with scenery and drama. Later, however, toward the middle of the seventeenth century, the oratorio ceased to be staged and became a work to be performed in a church or concert hall.

Perhaps the most famous oratorio is Handel's *Messiah,* written in 1742, near the end of the Baroque period. This work, like all the oratorios, had numerous movements for soloists, duets, quartets, chorus, and orchestra. Oratorios often have as many as 40-plus movements.

The works of Johann Sebastian Bach and George Frideric Handel embody all of the elements of music that culminated in the end of the Baroque period.

**Activity:**

1. Have you ever heard a cathedral's pipe organ? Can you imagine what Bach's or Handel's music might have sounded like to people hearing it for the first time? How would it have made them feel? Would it have surprised them in any way?

Name____________________________Date____________________________

# QUESTION COUNTDOWN

1. Who were two of the greatest composers in the Baroque period?

________________________________________________________

2. Where was Johann Sebastian Bach born?

________________________________________________________

3. This word describes a performer who has great technical ability on an instrument:

________________________________________________________

4. What is the name of a work for vocalists, chorus, and instrumentalists based on a poetic narrative of a dramatic nature?

________________________________________________________

5. What is the difference between a cantata and an opera?

________________________________________________________

6. Where was George Frideric Handel born?

________________________________________________________

7. Define the term *oratorio.*

________________________________________________________

8. Where were cantatas and oratorios generally performed?

________________________________________________________

9. What was Handel's most famous oratorio?

________________________________________________________

10. How many oratorios did Handel write?

________________________________________________________

# MUSIC IN THE CLASSICAL PERIOD (1750–1820)

**Classical music was designed to appeal to a wide-ranging audience.**

The term "classical music" is often a general term that is applied to any music that is not of the jazz, rock, or popular music styles. It applies more specifically, however, to the style of music that was composed in the eighteenth and early nineteenth centuries in Europe. The term "classical" during this time period was taken from art history, where the styles of art were influenced by ancient Greek and Roman sculptures. The important elements of music and art during the Classical period were the stresses on balance and clarity of structure.

There were four basic criteria that music of the Classical era needed in order to meet the needs and the desires of the public. (1) It needed to be universal, not limited by boundaries of countries or cities. The music of the Classical period needed to be able to communicate to people everywhere. (2) It was to have an aspect of nobility to it and, yet, be entertaining so as to meet the needs of the aristocracy and the middle class. (3) It needed to be expressive within the bounds of an established decorum. It was to express emotion and passion within the bounds of musical and social etiquette. (4) Music in the Classical period was natural and free of any technical complications. It had to be readily accessible to all ears: those of a trained musician and those of the common folk.

The three main composers of the Classical period were Franz Joseph Haydn (1732–1809), Wolfgang Amadeus Mozart (1756–1791), and Ludwig van Beethoven (1770–1827). Each of these composers had a very different style and approach to the composition of their music. During their lifetimes they saw a drastic shift in power from the aristocracy and the church to the middle class. An important development that occurred during the Classical period was the emancipation of the composer, and each of these composers represents different stages in that emancipation evolution.

Joseph Haydn chose to live and compose as a musical servant to a wealthy aristocratic family for most of his professional life. Mozart attempted to break away from this lifestyle, but perhaps because of his temperament, he was unable to be successful with this and died in poverty. Beethoven was the first successful major composer to completely break away from the service of an aristocratic family and make his living as a freelance composer, thereby setting one of many standards for the composers who would follow him.

**Activities:**

1. Research an important social or political event that occurred between 1750 and 1825. How could this event have affected the music world?

2. As a class, watch all or part of the movie *Amadeus* and discuss it.

Name_______________ Date_______________

# QUESTION COUNTDOWN

1. What styles of music do not generally fit under the term "classical music"?

2. The term "classical" specifically refers to the style of music from which centuries?

3. What type of history does the term "classical" refer to during the eighteenth and nineteenth centuries in Europe?

4. What are the two important elements of music and art during the Classical period?

5. One of the criteria of music in the Classical era was that it needed to be universal. Explain.

6. What type of people did music in the Classical period need to appeal to?

7. Who were the three main composers of the Classical period?

8. What is meant by the term "emancipation" of composers?

9. Of the three major composers in the Classical period, which of the three was most successful in freeing himself from patronage?

10. Which of the three composers of the Classical era died in poverty?

# THE WAR OF THE BUFFOONS

Opera continued to develop and gain a wider audience in the eighteenth century.

Opera in the eighteenth century was a much more developed art form than opera in the Baroque period. Since opera began in Italy, primarily with the works of Claudio Monteverdi, the Italians believed that they had a monopoly on that art form. The French had undertaken opera as a new art form and felt that serious opera was the only viable art form. The Italians, who had grown tired of using only serious subjects, believed that comic opera, called *opera buffa,* was a new and realistic art form.

In 1752 a troupe of Italian singers presented a comic opera entitled *La Serva padrona* (The Servant Mistress) by Giovanni Battista Pergolesi (1710–1736). This set off a dramatic reaction in France and caused what came to be known as the "war of the buffoons." The war that resulted was essentially a war of words between those who favored the traditional French court opera and those who saw in the Italian comic *opera buffa* a viable artistic outlet. The camp in favor of the French opera was headed by King Louis XV, Madame de Pompadour, and the aristocracy. The camp that was in favor of the Italian comic opera was headed by the queen and a group known as the encyclopedists, who favored the comic form because of its expressive melody and natural sentiment. In essence, the war of the buffoons was a contest between the rising middle-class—or bourgeois—art, and the falling aristocratic art.

Rousseau, though not a particularly accomplished composer, was one of the encyclopedists and wrote a short comic opera called *Le Devin du Village* (The Village Soothsayer) in 1752, that helped put Italian comic opera over the top and secured its place as a viable art form in eighteenth-century classical music.

An important composer of the eighteenth century was Christoph Willibald Gluck (1714–1787), who combined the elements of comic opera and the French courtly opera into what became the new operatic style of Europe. His efforts in combining the two forms created the foundation upon which Mozart and other future great opera composers would base their works.

**Activities:**

1. As a person in the eighteenth century, do you think that *opera buffa* or French opera should be the correct musical form? Why? Why do you consider the other form to be wrong?

2. Listen to a sample of each type of opera. Which type do you prefer? Why?

Name________________________________ Date________________________________________

# CROSSWORD PUZZLE

Use the clues below to complete the puzzle. Answers to the questions can be found in the narrative.

## ACROSS

2. Favored comic opera.
3. Italian comic opera.
6. Believed they had a monopoly on opera.
8. Leader of the group in favor of Italian comic opera.
12. Opposed comic opera.
15. Composer of *La Serva padrona.*
17. Leader of the group in favor of French opera.
19. He would be a great opera composer.
20. Traditional French ______ opera.
21. An important composer of eighteenth-century opera.

## DOWN

1. Synonym for rising middle class.
4. Opera began in the _______ Period.
5. The _______ Soothsayer.
7. 1752 comic opera.
9. Gluck combined the ______ of comic opera with French opera.
10. Composer of short comic opera called *Le Devin du Village.*
11. Opera in France was a new ______ form.
13. The wealthy and the nobility.
14. Not a real war, but a war of _______ .
16. War of the _______.
18. Believed that serious opera was the only viable art form.

 

# FRANZ JOSEPH HAYDN AND THE ESTERHAZYS

**Franz Joseph Haydn**

Franz Joseph Haydn was born in 1732 in a small village in lower Austria called Rohrau. He was the son of a wheelwright and began his musical career as a chorister in St. Stephen's Cathedral in Vienna. He remained there until he was 16 years old. When his voice changed, his career as a chorister came to an end. He then secured a dilapidated harpsichord, found himself an attic in Vienna, and began his compositional career. During his early years he was barely able to make a living as a teacher and accompanist and often joined bands of roving musicians who performed in the streets in Vienna. Because of this background in his formative years, Haydn would later incorporate into his compositions a great many of the folk tunes of Vienna and the region of Austria in which he grew up.

It wasn't long before Haydn attracted the notice of the aristocracy in Vienna. He was invited to live in the country house of a nobleman. This nobleman had a small group of musicians that functioned as an orchestra to him. For the next several years Haydn was able to experiment with different instruments and combinations of instruments as a part of this orchestra.

At the age of 29 in 1761, Haydn began his career with the Esterhazys, a family of Hungarian background who were famous for their patronage of the arts. This relationship would continue for nearly 30 years, the greater part of Haydn's creative career. The musicians who were acquired by the Esterhazys were among the finest in Europe, thus making the orchestra and any performances at the Esterhazys' court some of the best in all of Europe. Under Haydn's direction, the musical establishment of the Esterhazys included an orchestra, an opera company, a marionette theater, and a chapel. With the death of the prince, Haydn was released from the Esterhazys' service. He traveled to England twice—once in 1791 and again in 1794—where his music gained him great acclaim. When he returned to Austria, he was very well-off and laden with honor. He died in 1809 and was acknowledged throughout Europe as one of the premiere musicians of his time.

**Activities:**

1. Create an entry from Haydn's diary. Describe a typical day in Haydn's life.

2. Listen to excerpts from Haydn's *Surprise Symphony.* Did you notice anything surprising about it? What? Look up background information on the piece. Do you now have any new ideas for how it got its title?

Name____________________________ Date____________________________

# QUESTION COUNTDOWN

1. Where was Franz Joseph Haydn born in 1732?

_______________________________________________

2. Was Haydn's father a musician? If not, what line of work was he in?

_______________________________________________

3. Where did Haydn begin his musical career?

_______________________________________________

4. What happened at the age of 16 that ended his chorister career?

_______________________________________________

5. How did he make his living in his early years?

_______________________________________________

6. How would Haydn's background during his early years affect his compositions in later life?

_______________________________________________

7. What was the name of the family to which Haydn attached himself in 1761?

_______________________________________________

8. What was the quality of the musicians who were acquired by the Esterhazys?

_______________________________________________

9. What event precipitated the release of Haydn from the Esterhazys' service?

_______________________________________________

10. What country did he travel to twice—once in 1791 and again in 1794?

_______________________________________________

# AMADEUS—A CHILD PRODIGY

Wolfgang Amadeus Mozart

Wolfgang Amadeus Mozart was born in Salzburg, Austria, in 1756. He was the son of Leopold Mozart, a famous composer and violinist in the court of the Archbishop of Salzburg. Contrary to the career of Haydn, Mozart began his career before he was five years old. He was deemed a child prodigy. Mozart began composing before the age of five and performed in the court of the Empress Maria Theresa at the age of six. The following year, his father organized a performing tour for Mozart that would take him to Paris, London, and Munich. By the time the young Mozart was 13 years old, he had written sonatas, concertos, symphonies, religious works, and several operas. Before Mozart reached manhood, he had attained a mastery of all forms of his art. Mozart was a free spirit, however, and was more interested in developing his own pursuits as a freelance musician than he was in living under the traditional patronage system like Haydn. He made his patrons so unhappy with him that he was dismissed by the Archbishop. He then established himself in Vienna as a free artist.

While in Vienna, Mozart continued to pursue an official appointment and, at length, did receive an appointment from Emperor Joseph II. However, the Emperor appears to have only assigned him the simplest and most uninteresting tasks, such as composing dance music for the court balls.

In 1782 Mozart married Constance Weber. This marriage very much upset Mozart's father, who exercised tremendous control over the young Mozart, and it seems to have marked the liberation of Mozart from his domineering father. Constance, however, was not able to help Mozart in any way financially, and, having declared independence from his father, Mozart was cut off from the financial aid that his father might have given him. In addition, his attitude and lack of decorum with the aristocracy and those who would have asked him to compose for them caused him not to receive the remuneration that was his due owing to his genius and ability.

Mozart died at the age of 35 in 1791, virtually penniless and in many respects not particularly well known or highly acclaimed. It was not until years after his death that the works of Mozart began to be revived and performed with great regularity and Mozart gained the notoriety that he had sought throughout his life.

**Activities:**

1. Mozart wrote his first piece of music at the age of four. Try to compose a piece of music yourself. What did you find was difficult about it? How was it easy or fun to do?

2. Do you know a freelance artist, writer, or musician? What is his or her life like?

Name______________________________Date______________________________

# QUESTION COUNTDOWN

1. Where was Mozart born?

2. Who was Mozart's father, and what was his position?

3. At what age did Mozart begin his musical career?

4. List five types of musical pieces Mozart had written by age 13.

5. Instead of under the patronage system, how did Mozart want to work?

6. From whom did Mozart receive an appointment in Vienna?

7. How did Mozart break free from his father?

8. How did this break hurt Mozart?

9. Why wasn't Mozart employed more by the aristocracy to compose music?

10. When Mozart died, what was his station in life?

Name______________________________Date______________________________

# WORD UNSCRAMBLE

Unscramble these words and phrases that have to do with Mozart. Write the unscrambled words on the lines on the right.

1. SEORAP ____________________
2. ENSTSYEAROAPGMT ____________________
3. LEEEFANRC ____________________
4. PSMSREE ____________________
5. TZMLORDALEPOO ____________________
6. SAPIR ____________________
7. ARNWAZMGOGOTLF ____________________
8. OJREEPHROSPEM ____________________
9. PCOESMOR ____________________
10. RDIHPGILDYCO ____________________
11. HMIUCN ____________________
12. GZLBURAS ____________________
13. ICOARASTYCR ____________________
14. ZOSHFTAERMTAR ____________________
15. EANNVI ____________________
16. HSYOMEINPS ____________________
17. AITEONNPTMP ____________________
18. NSRBCEONECTEWA ____________________
19. DONLON ____________________
20. SYRMETA ____________________

# LUDWIG van BEETHOVEN: A STORMY LIFE

Ludwig van Beethoven

Ludwig van Beethoven was born in 1770 in the city of Bonn, Germany, in what is called the Rhineland. His father and grandfather were singers at the court of the local prince, but the family situation was most unhappy. Beethoven's father was addicted to alcohol, and Ludwig was forced at an early age to assume the support of his mother and two younger brothers. At age 11 he was the assistant organist in the court chapel, and a year later, he became harpsichordist in the court orchestra. When he was 17, he visited Vienna and played for Mozart. Mozart was impressed by Beethoven and remarked to his friends, "Keep an eye on him—he will make a noise in the world someday."

At age 22 arrangements were made for Beethoven to study with Haydn in Vienna. Their relationship was strained, however, mostly because Haydn was ruffled by Beethoven's volcanic temperament and free spirit. His abilities as a pianist earned him great respect and notoriety among the aristocracy, and he was welcomed into the great homes of some of the most powerful patrons in Vienna.

Beethoven, though often moody and temperamental, was able to function well under a modified patronage system. This meant that he was not directly attached to any particular princely court; rather, the aristocrats of Vienna helped him financially through gifts or lesson payments. He was also aided by the emergence of an upper class who appreciated the music that had only been heard by royalty and the wealthy in times past. Another development that helped Beethoven break free of the patronage system was the greatly increased amount of music publishing. This allowed his music to be performed and heard throughout Europe.

When Beethoven was in his late 20s, however, he began to exhibit symptoms of one of the most dreadful curses that a musician could ever face: Beethoven was going deaf. By 1802 his hearing was nearly gone, and he was so distraught that he thought many times of taking his own life. However, Beethoven found the strength to endure this horrific challenge that was given him and continued for nearly 25 years to both compose and conduct many of his own pieces. In fact, many of Beethoven's most famous and popular compositions were composed at a time in the composer's life when he was not able to hear them be performed. He could only hear them in his head. An active conductor and composer throughout his life, Beethoven would never hear the applause that was his for many of the works he composed.

A carriage ride in inclement weather brought on an attack of dropsy that proved fatal. Ludwig van Beethoven died in 1827 at the age of 57, revered by the greatest composers of his time. For at least a hundred years following Beethoven's death, composers looked to his compositions as the standard of excellence for their own.

Name____________________________Date____________________________

# QUESTION COUNTDOWN

1. Who was born in 1770 in the city of Bonn, Germany?

____________________________________________

2. What is that area of Germany often referred to as?

____________________________________________

3. What did his father and grandfather do?

____________________________________________

4. At age 11, what was his job?

____________________________________________

5. At age 12, what was his new job?

____________________________________________

6. Who said this about Beethoven: "Keep an eye on him—he will make a noise in the world someday"?

____________________________________________

7. Why did Haydn not particularly care for Beethoven?

____________________________________________

8. What development during Beethoven's life enabled his music to be performed and heard throughout Europe?

____________________________________________

9. When Beethoven was in his late twenties, what dreadful curse afflicted him?

____________________________________________

10. Following Beethoven's death, why did composers still look to his compositions?

____________________________________________

# MUSIC IN THE ROMANTIC PERIOD (1820–1900)

**Composers of the Romantic period were able to write music for their own purposes.**

The term "romantic" is often used to describe feelings of love between people. But in the case of Romantic music, it has very little to do with that type of definition. The Romantic period in history came at a time of great development and strife in the world. It coincided with the Industrial Revolution, which created a tremendous amount of social and economic change.

The Romantic period stressed emotion, imagination, and individualism. As with many of the periods of music history, this period was a reaction or a rebellion against the period that preceded it—the Classical period. Composers in the Romantic period were free from the bondage of having to work for the aristocracy that many of the earlier composers felt, and they were therefore able to compose music more for their own individual and egocentric purposes. However, because they were not able to make as much money as the earlier composers did when they worked for the aristocracy, the composers of the Romantic period often worked on the side as teachers, conductors, music critics, or soloists. Most of the music of the Romantic period was written for the middle class by middle-class composers.

Several elements set Romantic music apart from music that had come before it and would come after it. The Romantic composer put a great deal of emphasis on self-expression and his or her own individual style. Whereas in the Classical period composers felt that they needed to write music that was understood and liked by everyone, composers in the Romantic period felt strongly that they should compose music that satisfied their own desires and needs as people and as individuals.

The subjects of the compositions often dealt with fantastic or dream-like characters. Nature also was very important to composers of the Romantic period in showing the difference between the individual man versus all of nature. Nationalism was a very important aspect of music in the Romantic period. Nationalism is a theme of specific national identity. The composers would use folk songs, legends, and the country's history as the subjects for these compositions.

In addition to nationalism, many composers in the Romantic period wrote music that dealt with far-away countries and lands and their exotic natures. Composers in Europe would write of peoples and music of Africa, the Mediterranean, or the Orient. One of the most important elements in all of Romantic music is its programmatic nature. Program music has a specific story, idea, or scene that the composer wants to portray through music.

Perhaps the greatest of all the differences between Romantic music and the music that had gone before was the change from miniature or smaller forms to the focus and emphasis on larger forms of music. Symphonies, concertos, chorales, and oratorios all became much longer pieces of music than they had been previously. It might take 15–20 minutes to perform all three or four movements of a piece that was written in the Classical period, but a Romantic symphony could take as long as two full hours.

Name__________________________ Date__________________________

# WORD SEARCH

Find the terms listed below. They may be printed in the puzzle horizontally, vertically, diagonally, or backward. All of the words are associated with the narrative in some way.

```
Q N Q Z J R Q D U D C U S M O Q O W A K
L C I R T N E C O G E F E R P S P P A E
G Y V I N O I T U L O V E R Q W S H D X
J H T F A N U X G I V A Y S M Z A E F C
D P S Q J Y O T U F Z C F A U T M K A I
W R I C M O D I Z O U U T N S E N B X T
X O O Q O I I T L L K X K A I L E Z O N
N G L B G N D E S L L J T T C Y W S Y A
A R O Y L F D D N Q E H Q U C T M Y I M
T A S L C N O U L P F B Z R R S S M Y O
I M N S K E Q E C E S A E E I T A P S R
O M X W F E P M R T C J O R T G J H A K
N A J P O U I O U E O L Y T I V J O T F
A T R B L A A T U O H R A N C C F N N S
L I S W K N N I J I I C A S I C E Y A Z
I C K G S V X O B D T T A Q S V M O F C
S A G R O Y V N V Z I J R E A C T I O N
M B F Z N P O R I O C W I C T O F V M V
W H S Z G N A G N L N S Q E F U H W N V
N J L Q M S I L A U D I V I D N I X N X
```

1. conductor
2. fantasy
3. individualism
4. nationalism
5. reaction
6. Romantic
7. symphony
8. egocentric
9. folk song
10. middle class
11. nature
12. rebellion
13. soloist
14. teacher
15. emotion
16. imagination
17. music critic
18. programmatic
19. revolution
20. style

# SCHUBERT'S *UNFINISHED SYMPHONY*

**Franz Peter Schubert**

Franz Peter Schubert was born in 1797 in a small town not far from Vienna, Austria. He began his musical training on a violin with his father, and later learned piano from an older brother. When he was 11, Schubert started singing in one of the court chapels in Vienna. He began regular music studies at the boarding school there, and he became a violinist in the school orchestra. He composed his first symphony in 1813 at the age of 16. During the 17 years between 1811 and 1828 (from age 14 until his death), Schubert composed about 1,000 works. Of these, nine were symphonies.

Schubert is considered one of the earliest composers of the Romantic type of symphony. He is particularly noted for what has come to be known as *The Unfinished Symphony.* This was his eighth symphony, written in 1822. He was 25 years old at the time, but the work was not performed until 1865, 43 years after his death. It was nicknamed *The Unfinished Symphony* because it has only two movements. Most of the symphonies of that time had three or four movements. No symphony of the Classical or Romantic period had only two movements, unless, for some reason, the composer had chosen not to complete the work. Schubert, however, apparently believed that the symphony could stand alone with only two movements. Since he died at the early age of 31, he never had an opportunity to change his mind later in life.

In his short life, Franz Schubert gained the respect and admiration of the people who performed and heard his works. He was never a very wealthy man. When he died, his last wish was to be buried near the great Ludwig van Beethoven. That wish was granted, and on his tombstone was written: "The art of music here entombed a rich possession that even far fairer hopes."

**Activities:**

1. Listen to part or all of Schubert's *Unfinished Symphony.* How is it different from other symphonies from that time period?

2. Schubert wanted to be buried near Beethoven because he admired him so much. Who do you admire? Why?

3. Why is it helpful to begin studying music at an early age? Do you or any of your classmates enjoy playing a musical instrument? You may want to play a short solo for the class.

Name______________________________ Date______________________________

# QUESTION COUNTDOWN

1. What was the name of the composer who was born in 1797, not far from Vienna, Austria?

______________________________

2. On what instrument did Schubert begin his training?

______________________________

3. At the age of 16, what did Schubert compose?

______________________________

4. Approximately how many works did Schubert compose between 1811 and 1828?

______________________________

5. Of what type of symphony was Schubert considered to be one of the earliest composers?

______________________________

6. What was the title of the symphony Schubert composed that consisted of only two movements?

______________________________

7. How many movements did most symphonies have during the Classical and early Romantic periods?

______________________________

8. How old was Schubert when he died?

______________________________

9. What was Schubert's last wish?

______________________________

10. How many symphonies did Schubert compose during his lifetime?

______________________________

# FRANZ LISZT: THE PIANO TERMINATOR

**Franz Liszt**

Franz Liszt was born in 1811 in Hungary. At the age of 11 he moved to Vienna. There he met Schubert and Beethoven while studying music. While he was in his teens and twenties, he lived in Paris. While there, Liszt heard the great violin virtuoso, Paganini, and declared that he wanted to be as great a virtuoso on the piano as Paganini was on the violin. He had been performing on concert stages already, but at age 19 he withdrew from the concert stage for a few years and practiced from 8 to 12 hours a day. When he came out of seclusion, Franz Liszt became one of the greatest pianists of his time. He toured Europe for eight years, playing most of his own piano music and receiving tremendous acclaim.

Liszt was known as a great performer who could go through as many as two or three pianos in a concert. The pianos of that time were not nearly as sturdy as the pianos that we have today, and Liszt was a very physically strong player. Often, by the end of one relatively long piece of music they would have to replace the piano that he had been playing with a new one so that he could continue his concert. This knack that Liszt had for destroying pianos gave him a reputation that would have earned him a name in our day as a piano "terminator."

When Liszt was 36, he decided to no longer travel and perform as a soloist. Instead, he wanted to stay in one place and become a conductor. During this time he composed and conducted many of his own orchestral pieces as well as works of his contemporaries such as Berlioz, Schumann, and Wagner. He was also an active music critic and wrote several books.

In his last years, Liszt wrote music that was unique and curious. It showed hints of what might be coming in twentieth-century music. However, these works went very much unappreciated, and Franz Liszt died in 1886. Of him the Grand Duke of Weimar said, "Liszt was what a prince ought to be."

**Activities:**

1. Describe something that you think you could practice 8 to 12 hours a day for several years. How would you feel about going into seclusion and spending that much time practicing?

2. If possible, as a class, go to a live piano recital or concert, especially if pieces by Liszt are on the program. As an alternative, invite an accomplished guest pianist to perform a Liszt piece for the class.

Name______________________________ Date______________________________

# QUESTION COUNTDOWN

1. In what country was Franz Liszt born?

______________________________________________________________

2. Whom did he meet when he moved to Vienna?

______________________________________________________________

3. During his teens and twenties, where did Liszt live?

______________________________________________________________

4. Who was the great violin virtuoso that Liszt heard in Paris?

______________________________________________________________

5. How many hours a day did Liszt practice before he came out of seclusion?

______________________________________________________________

6. Why did Liszt go through so many pianos in a concert?

______________________________________________________________

7. What did Liszt want to do at the age of 36 when he retired from performing as a soloist?

______________________________________________________________

8. In addition to his own orchestral pieces, whose works did he conduct?

______________________________________________________________

9. What were some of Liszt's other activities in his later life in addition to his conducting?

______________________________________________________________

10. How were the works he wrote in his later years received?

______________________________________________________________

# ROMANTIC OPERA: BIGGER MUST BE BETTER

**Tragic stories were often the themes of Romantic operas.**

By the middle of the Romantic period, opera had changed drastically from its style during the Baroque period. It had spread from being primarily an Italian-dominated art form to an art form that was respected and built on in many countries throughout the Western world. The three main countries where opera continued to thrive in varying forms and degrees of development were Italy, France, and Germany.

Some of the great composers of Italian opera in the Romantic period were Rossini, Donizetti, Bellini, Verdi, and Puccini. The main figure in French romantic opera was George Bizet, and the two main composers of German Romantic opera were Carl Maria von Weber and Richard Wagner.

Opera had always been known as an art form that employed huge forces, larger-than-life sets, and dazzling costumes and special effects. During the Romantic period, the emphasis was placed on nature, fantasy, and dreams, and all of the elements of opera became even larger and more dazzling. The music in the Romantic period was also more refined. It developed a larger ensemble complemented by newcomers to the orchestra such as trombones, tubas, and a large battery of percussion instruments.

Opera composers throughout history have been drawn to tragic themes. Loss of love, loss of life (or both), loss of power —all contribute to a better story line. As a backdrop to these themes, some of the most beautiful music in all of history was composed during the Romantic era.

## Activities:

1. Make up a tragedy as a story for a nineteenth-century opera.

2. Watch or listen to excerpts from Bizet's *Carmen* and/or Verdi's *La Traviata.* Have your teacher tell you the basic story line. What do you think of Romantic opera?

3. As a class, write and perform an opera using some of the elements of opera as discussed in this chapter.

Name________________________________Date________________________________

# WORD SEARCH

Find the terms listed below. They may be printed in the puzzle horizontally, vertically, diagonally, or backward. All of the words are associated with the narrative in some way.

```
L D V V X N O I S S U C R E P Z W N H O
Y Q Y R Z R E N G A W D R A H C I R R K
G S Q F J E L A C H W Y F A N T A S Y P
A P I R R A V P Y W S M A E R D I X O F
P E Q E Q Y X G J O E Z Y Z V E T S Y M
E C N A R F P K C N J B G C L M A E R E
Q I P D F N T Z I I J Q E N U T L N H L
X A N W Q B C P T W T S B R M W Y O I A
T L A S Q W G U T E Y N A M R E G B B R
P E R I S Q E C E C W G A W V F X M R G
Z F E Y T Z O C Z O T G F M P L O O O E
N F P U W R R I I S U Q T P O F B R S R
Q E O F X Z G N N B B F Q C E R P T S T
J C X K X B E I O Q A T R A G I C G I H
Z T X S Z G B V D Y S L R G S X X V N A
E S Y Q O U I B B E L L I N I A B S I N
U O I D A Z Z L I N G C O S T U M E S L
R V O W Q C E B F N E R U T A N N O L I
X N S M M X T U B D Y F A C T Y V T Q F
O D S I D R E V H M J C K Q Q S F D J E
```

1. Bellini
2. dreams
3. George Bizet
4. larger than life
5. percussion
6. Romantic
7. tragic
8. Verdi
9. dazzling costumes
10. fantasy
11. Germany
12. nature
13. Puccini
14. Rossini
15. trombones
16. Weber
17. Donizetti
18. France
19. Italy
20. opera
21. Richard Wagner
22. special effects
23. tubas

# RICHARD WAGNER: THE EGOCENTRIC

Richard Wagner

Richard Wagner was born in Leipzig, Germany, in 1813. He was the son of a clerk in the city police court who died when Richard was only six months old. Wagner was a precocious child who began showing an early interest in literature. He wrote his first tragedy in free Shakespearean style at the age of 14. As a musician, Wagner began studying piano at the age of 12 but never really developed into a fine performer on the instrument. However, by the time he was 19, several of his works had been performed publicly. And at the age of 20, he began his professional career as a musician when he became the chorus master for a nearby theater. While there and in several positions that followed, Wagner began composing operas.

Throughout Wagner's life he had a very difficult time having his works performed. The main reason for this was because so many of his works called for enormous forces—huge orchestras and grand-scale scenery—most of which was not available at even the largest opera houses in Europe.

Wagner married in his mid-twenties and was soon appointed as a conductor to the king of Saxony in Germany. For the next six years, Wagner was very busy composing his own operas and producing operas of other composers. However, because Wagner was involved in a revolutionary uprising in 1848 and 1849, he was forced to flee and was exiled to Switzerland. While there he wrote two very important books: *The Art Work of the Future* (1850), and *Opera and Drama* (1851). Both described Wagner's approach to opera. He believed that this form should be different from the operas that were being composed at the time. Wagner believed that the world revolved around him and that most of the world did not understand him. Because of this egocentric attitude, Wagner often alienated people around him.

While in Switzerland, Wagner began laying the foundations for many of his later works that would gain him great acclaim. In particular, he began his work for four music dramas that were all part of what was called *Der Ring des Nibelungen* (The Ring of the Nibelungs). Each of the four sections of this epic lasts three to five hours, and the entire epic must be put on over a four-day period.

Wagner's ideas on music would set the stage for much of what was to come in the twentieth century, and his works will always be noted for their grand scale and use of extremely large forces. Wagner died in Venice, Italy, in 1883 at the age of 70.

**Activity:**

1. Wagner uses recurring themes throughout his music to represent characters or ideas. Create or describe a melody to represent each of the characters in a short story or children's story book (such as *Goldilocks and the Three Bears*).

Name______________________Date______________________

# CROSSWORD PUZZLE

Use the clues below to complete the puzzle. Answers to the questions can be found in the narrative.

1 2 3 4 5 6 7 8 9 10 11 12 13 14 15 16 17 18 19 20

**ACROSS**

3. Married in mid-_____.
5. His first play was a _____.
7. *The Art Work of the* _____.
10. Death place
12. He began studying this instrument at the age of 12.
14. *Der Ring des* _____.
15. Born in Leipzig, Germany
18. Place of exile
20. _____ uprising.

**DOWN**

1. To whom was Wagner appointed conductor?
2. At age 20 he was a chorus _____ for a nearby theater.
4. Self-centered
6. Four _____ dramas
8. Opposite of tiny
9. City Wagner was born in
11. Showed an early interest in this art form
13. A child smart beyond his years
16. *Opera and*_____.
17. Musical form Wagner dealt with
19. Long story

# IMPRESSIONISM AND EXPRESSIONISM

When people walk on soft soil, they leave an impression or a footprint. When a comedian does an impression of someone, he does a likeness of that person. When you meet someone for the first time, after he has left he leaves an impression on you. In all of these instances, the actual person or foot or face is not present, but it has left an impression in your mind or in your eyes as you see it or as you think about it. So it is with the music of the Impressionist period that occurred in the late 1800s.

**Impressionistic music, like Impressionistic art, was designed to create a certain mood or atmosphere.**

Impressionistic music was an offspring of Impressionistic art. French artists such as Claude Monet and August Renoir painted pictures that were not actual trees and were not actual scenes of water or of gardens, but were impressions of those. They were short strokes or flecks of colored patches that when viewed closely were nothing but formless collections of color, but when viewed from a distance they became recognizable forms. These painters were concerned mostly with the effects of light, color, and atmosphere. So, too, the composers who tried to copy this style of art in their music were more concerned with a certain mood or atmosphere and tried to recreate that in their music. The most famous and well-known composer of the Impressionists was a Frenchman named Claude Debussy. The titles of some of his works show how in his music he attempts to paint a picture. "Reflections in the Water," "Clouds," and "Sounds and Perfumes Swirl in the Evening Air" are examples of this type of musical painting.

Expressionism was a reaction against Impressionism. It occurred primarily in Germany among German painters, writers, and composers. The idea in Expressionism was to deliberately distort something so as to shock the audience and to communicate tension and anguish. They chose not to depict the typical beautiful scenes that the Impressionists did. Their focus was more on the inner self or inner feelings than on outward appearances. Expressionist painters were Ernst Ludwig Kirchner, Emil Nolde, and Oskar Kokoschka. Some of the composers of Expressionist music were Arnold Schönberg, Alban Berg, and Anton von Webern. These composers deliberately turned away from traditional styles of composition and sought for new ways to express the inner turmoil that they felt and believed everyone else felt.

## Activities:

1. Draw a picture that uses the ideas of Impressionism.

2. Draw a picture that uses the ideas of Expressionism.

Name______________________________Date______________________________________

# QUESTION COUNTDOWN

1. When a person walks on soft soil, what is left behind?

_______________________________________________

2. Who were two of the French Impressionist artists?

_______________________________________________

3. How did these artists and others like them create the impressions in their paintings?

_______________________________________________

4. Who was the most famous and well-known composer of Impressionistic music?

_______________________________________________

5. What were the titles of two of his Impressionistic works?

_______________________________________________

6. What were composers more concerned with in their music?

_______________________________________________

7. In what country did Expressionism primarily occur?

_______________________________________________

8. Who were three of the Expressionistic composers?

_______________________________________________

9. What did Expressionism deliberately set out to do?

_______________________________________________

10. Composers and artists in Expressionism sought for new ways to express something that occurred within people. What was that something?

_______________________________________________

_______________________________________________

# MUSIC IN THE TWENTIETH CENTURY

Jazz became the popular music of the early twentieth century.

With the dawning of a new age in time came the dawning of a new age in music. The composers of music in the twentieth century sought to completely abandon the traditional styles, forms, and sounds that constituted all of the music that had gone before them. The composers of the twentieth century desperately wanted to break out of the molds that they felt cast into. And so the music of the twentieth century has a great variety of styles and new sounds. Many of these sounds were not well received when they first appeared.

Perhaps the most startling development in music was the complete abandonment of traditional harmony. Composers now sought to use all 12 of the tones in music at one time and in one piece in order to best depict what they felt inside. This was so startling to music critics and audiences at the turn of the century that these works were booed in concert and were strongly criticized as being nothing but noise.

Simultaneous with this development was the advent of a new style called "jazz." This would become the "popular" music of the early twentieth century and would eventually lead into modern rock and much of the popular music that is enjoyed today. The technological developments that occurred at the beginning of the twentieth century with electricity and electronic gadgets led to the first sounds of electronic music—music composed specifically for electronic instruments such as synthesizers.

The music of the twentieth century is new and sometimes alarming. It has taken the world by storm and has led to the popular music that is enjoyed today. An interesting thing to note is that in the last 15 years there has been a reaction against the music of the early twentieth century—the atonal music or music where all 12 tones are used in a composition. The movement has taken much of the classical music of today back to traditional harmonies and traditional sounds, such as those that would have been heard in the eighteenth and nineteenth centuries.

**Activities:**

1. Listen to an example of twentieth-century music. How do you feel about this type of music?

2. Individually or as a class, create a 12-tone composition. If possible, try playing it on classroom instruments.

3. Invite a musician from the community to demonstrate synthesizers and other forms of electronic music for the class.

Name________________________________Date________________________________

# WORD SCRAMBLE

Unscramble these words and phrases that have to do with music in the twentieth century. Write the unscrambled words on the lines on the right.

1. NWINDAG ______________________
2. TDMPOSLENVEE ______________________
3. NHRESITYZSE ______________________
4. SITOTASEYFLREVY ______________________
5. DINATIRTALO ______________________
6. DEWSNNSUO ______________________
7. NOTADMNABEN ______________________
8. UPAMLIUSPOCR ______________________
9. ROCMRNDKOE ______________________
10. LCLHATONCIEGO ______________________
11. NTNEETIWYETRCTUH ______________________
12. NGWEAE ______________________
13. TICSCLUNMOREICE ______________________
14. AZJZ ______________________
15. NMTISAACLOU ______________________
16. TNVWSOEETLE ______________________
17. CIOSMIOTONP ______________________
18. YNOMRAH ______________________
19. YIOSLADDAITSTENL ______________________

# SCHÖNBERG AND ATONALITY

**Arnold Schönberg**

Arnold Schönberg was born in Vienna in 1874 and was almost an entirely self-taught musician. He began his career as a bank clerk but lost his job at the age of 21 and decided at that time to devote himself to music. Around 1908, Schönberg began composing works that were drastically different from anything that had been composed up to that time. These compositions were *atonal,* meaning that they lacked a key signature. These compositions used all of the 12 tones. When one heard the works of Arnold Schönberg, one could not say necessarily that this piece began in the key of C Major and ended in the key of C Major (often indicated by beginning on C and ending on C).

The works that Arnold Schönberg composed were met with a great deal of hostility because they went against everything that had been taught and heard and performed until that time. But Schönberg was certain that this was the new direction that music should take in the twentieth century, and he persisted. It wasn't long before his works began to be well received and people began to try to understand what he was trying to do. With this understanding came an acceptance, and the acceptance led to the musical world's embrace of this new style of composition.

Arnold Schönberg was greatly influential on two of his young theory students: Alban Berg and Anton von Webern. Both of these composers, along with Schönberg, constitute the main composers of the Expressionist period. Through their works, these composers sought to use the ideals of the Expressionist painters and writers—that of distortion and grotesque disfigurement—to express the feelings, turmoil, and tension that they felt were in each of us. The works of Arnold Schönberg forever changed the world of music.

**Activities:**

1. What world events were occurring near the beginning of the twentieth century that may have affected composers such as Arnold Schönberg and their compositions?

2. Individually or as a class, create your own free-form atonal compositions.

3. Listen to a recording of Schönberg's cantata *A Survivor From Warsaw.* Express verbally or in written form how this piece made you feel.

Name_______________________________ Date_______________________________

# CROSSWORD PUZZLE

Use the clues below to complete the puzzle. Answers to the questions can be found in the narrative.

## ACROSS

2. Sharps and flats equal the ______ _____.
6. One of Schönberg's young theory students (first name).
7. How Arnold Schönberg learned music.
8. First composer of atonality.
11. Schönberg's first job.
13. An ideal of Expressionism.
14. Schönberg's first name.
16. Young theory _____.
18. Not minor but _____.
19. Understanding becomes ______.

## DOWN

1. Expressionism shows the feelings of ____.
3. City in which Schönberg was born.
4. Another of Schönberg's young theory students (first name).
5. The style these composers represent.
6. Type of music Schönberg composed.
9. Tonal "middle."
10. How different were Schönberg's early works?
12. The meaning of atonal: absence of ____.
15. One who writes music.
17. Twelve _____.

# THE JAZZ SCENE

**The clarinet, trumpet, and trombone were some of the solo instruments featured in jazz.**

While Schönberg and his colleagues were changing the sounds of classical music in Europe, a new style was developing in America known as "jazz." Jazz music combines the traditional harmony of European music, the rhythms and percussion and a style known as "call and response" of western Africa, and the fresh new style of playing known as "ragtime" from America. Scott Joplin was the leading ragtime composer and performer of the early twentieth century. Some of his most famous pieces included the "Maple Leaf Rag" and "The Entertainer." Jazz was also influenced by the "blues," which is a style of vocal music that came from the African-Americans and can be traced to the slave work songs.

The earliest jazz groups consisted of a rhythm section (piano, string bass, a drummer with a snare drum and cymbals, and sometimes a banjo or guitar) that kept the beat and provided the chords or the harmonies over which the other horns or singers played or sang. The main solo instruments of jazz included the coronet or trumpet, the saxophone, piano, clarinet, and trombone. The very heart of jazz is its improvisational nature. This, perhaps more than anything else in its nature, sets it apart from traditional European or classical music. Often in jazz the musicians take a simple melody, play it through once, and then improvise on that melody, changing it, adding notes to it, and sometimes going completely away from the melody. The Dixieland band, which was the main type of group in jazz from 1900 to 1917, originated in New Orleans. It included the rhythm section that we talked about, as well as a coronet or trumpet, clarinet, and trombone.

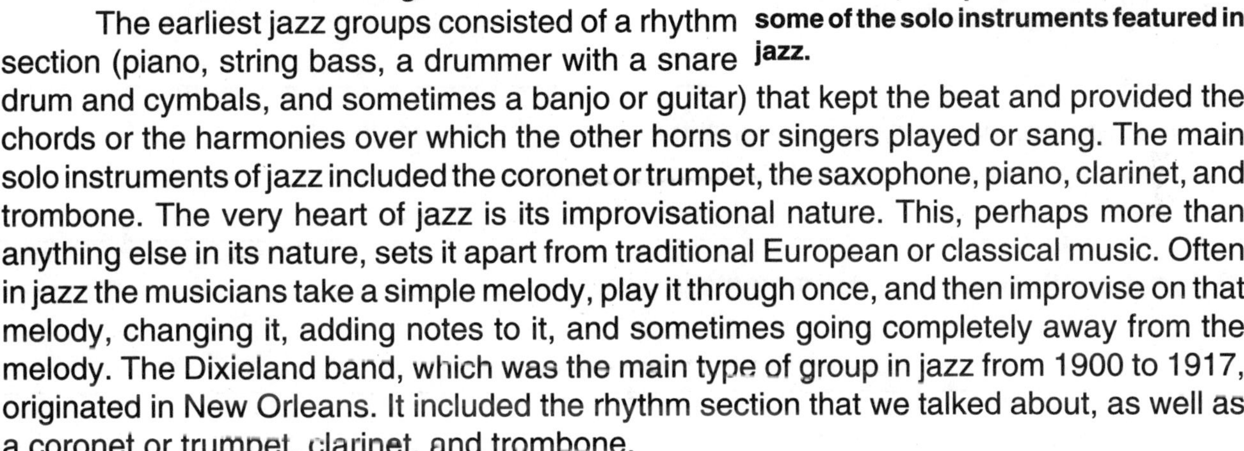

The center of jazz moved from New Orleans to Chicago, Illinois, in the early 1920s. There, a new style of jazz developed known as "swing." The swing era ran from about 1930 to 1945, and during this time "big bands" developed. These bands had a rhythm section and three woodwind sections: the saxophones, the trumpets, and trombones. Typically there would be three or four saxophones, three trombones, and three trumpets. Some of the most important names in the big band era were Count Basie, Glenn Miller, Tommy Dorsey, Duke Ellington, and Benny Goodman.

Early in the 1940s a new style of jazz began to develop that was called "bebop." In this style of music the emphasis was placed on solo playing, so there were many *quartets* (groups of four players) or *quintets* (groups of five players). They usually had a piano, bass, and drums, and a solo horn player. This style of music emphasized fast, lively rhythms and fluid solos by the players. Some of the most famous performers of bebop were Dizzy Gillespie and Charlie Parker.

Bebop remained popular into the early 1960s. Then jazz saw a resurgence in big band music with such notables as Stan Kenton and Maynard Ferguson. The jazz music that we hear today is sometimes very different from the jazz music that we would have heard back in the 1920s. Most of this is due to the revolution and development of electronic music and electronic instruments. Still, the very heart of jazz is and will always be the element of improvisation and spontaneous performance.

Name_____________________________Date_________________________________

# QUESTION COUNTDOWN

1. What was the new style of music developing in America?

_______________________________________________________________________

2. Who was the leading composer and performer of ragtime in the early twentieth century?

_______________________________________________________________________

3. List two of his most famous compositions.

_______________________________________________________________________

4. Where did the style of vocal music known as the "blues" originate?

_______________________________________________________________________

5. What are the instruments that constitute a jazz rhythm section?

_______________________________________________________________________

6. What are the main solo instruments in jazz?

_______________________________________________________________________

7. Where did Dixieland jazz originate?

_______________________________________________________________________

8. When Dixieland moved from New Orleans, what city became the center of jazz?

_______________________________________________________________________

9. Who were some of the most important names in the big band era?

_______________________________________________________________________

10. What is the most important element of jazz?

_______________________________________________________________________

Name________________________________Date________________________________

# WORD SEARCH

Find the terms listed below. They may be printed in the puzzle horizontally, vertically, diagonally, or backward. All of the words are associated with the narrative in some way.

```
Q L E N J R S O L O S L G S X R I Y G U
R A G U X U G B Z J L S K E G R T B T C
K N D O N O I T C E S M H T Y H R B A X
E O U P A M E R I C A M B F C M V I G A
F I K Y G Q W L G N R H L R A K G G D D
E T E Q S Z U N V Y E X E A C Q I B N X
L A E I N B L U E S U I Y E X U Y A A R
W S L M A O S W I N G V I D B A K N L C
S I L Y E I B Y N W Y P Q K F R S D E O
C V I A L S T T D F S E K W R T K S I U
O O N Z R B T F Y E N W I D A E U U X N
T R G S O E G E L I X E U I T T X A I T
T P T R W W A L T Q O P W E G S X C D B
J M O V E B I Q F N E J A Z Z R E I H A
O I N I N G R A G T I M E M Z M Z R V S
P N H S Y F K P N X A U P P W A E F G I
L X D Z X C H I C A G O Q M R B A A C E
I V Z T X A E I Q H J Y A H W T A H R J
N I V E X Q M B E B O P T M G M J E F S
D E Q T Z H T V C S N Y T Y M D D L N Q
```

1. Africa
2. America
3. bebop
4. big bands
5. blues
6. Chicago
7. Count Basie
8. Dixieland
9. Dizzy Gillespie
10. Duke Ellington
11. improvisational
12. jazz
13. New Orleans
14. quartets
15. quintets
16. ragtime
17. rhythm section
18. Scott Joplin
19. solos
20. swing

# ROCK AND ROLL AND BEYOND

Elvis Presley

Rock and roll "happened" in the mid-1950s. It took America by storm, then Europe, then the world. Its origins lie in a combination of rhythm and blues, jazz, and country-western music. The earliest known song that represents rock and roll is the song by Bill Hayley and His Comets entitled "Rock Around the Clock" (1954). Soon after that song came out, a young man from Memphis, Tennessee, known as Elvis Presley hit the scene and reigned for nearly 20 years as the "king" of rock and roll.

This new style of music captivated the young audiences in America in the 1950s. It was, for them, a form of rebellion and a way to break out of the molds that their parents had set for them. In 1964 a little-known group known as "The Beatles" came on an American tour. They became, in a very short period of time, the most well-known and successful rock band in history. Throughout the 1960s African-American rock music was known as "soul" music. It got its name from the emphasis that these tunes placed on gospel origins and heartfelt words.

Throughout the '60s, '70s, and '80s, rock has come to be a term that acts as an umbrella under which an incredible variety of styles and sounds coexists. So strong has rock's influence been that composers have sought to incorporate elements of rock and roll in musicals, pieces for choirs, church music, and symphonies. Rock music, like jazz, country-western, and all the other styles of music, has taken the elements of music from the past and combined them in new and different ways to create an independent identity.

It is impossible to predict what will happen in the future. There are composers today who are hearkening back to the music of the past, and many composers today are desperately seeking to be the Mozarts or Schönbergs of the future. Only time will tell what music will bring to us, but rest assured that we will hear it loud and clear.

**Activities:**

1. As a class, discuss the similarities and differences of rock and roll, jazz, and rhythm and blues.

2. As a class, discuss your favorite styles of music and why you prefer them to others.

3. Interview your parents. Ask question such as: when were you born?, what type of music did you listen to when you where my age?, were you around when rock and roll came on the scene?, and so on. Hand in the questions and responses, and have the teacher read them aloud. Then, try to guess whose parents gave which responses.

Name______________________________Date______________________________

# QUESTION COUNTDOWN

1. In what country did rock and roll begin?

______________________________________________________________

2. What three styles of music were combined to create rock and roll?

______________________________________________________________

3. What group performed a song entitled "Rock Around the Clock" in 1954?

______________________________________________________________

4. Who came out of Memphis, Tennessee, and was named the "king" of rock and roll?

______________________________________________________________

5. Why was rock music so popular with young people in the 1950s?

______________________________________________________________

6. What group came to America in 1964?

______________________________________________________________

7. Where did "soul" music get its name?

______________________________________________________________

8. Rock has been incorporated into a number of different forms of music. List them.

______________________________________________________________

9. How was rock music similar to jazz and other styles of music?

______________________________________________________________

10. After America, where was rock most popular?

______________________________________________________________

Name____________________________ Date__________________________________

# REVIEW QUESTIONS

1. What are the approximate years of the Middle Ages? ____________________

2. What are the approximate years of the Renaissance period? ____________________

3. What are the approximate years of the Baroque period? ____________________

4. What are the approximate years of the Classical period? ____________________

5. What are the approximate years of the Romantic period? ____________________

6. What are the approximate years of the Twentieth Century period? ____________________

7. How did Gregorian Chants receive their name? ____________________

8. What is polyphony, and how does it differ from monophony? ____________________

9. What were the troubadours, trouvères, and jongleurs? ____________________

10. What is the difference between "new art" and "old art"? ____________________

11. Who was Josquin des Prez? ____________________

12. What is the difference between sacred and secular music? ____________________

13. What is a motet? ____________________

14. What country were Palestrina and Gabrieli from? ____________________

15. What major accomplishment is attributed to Claudio Monteverdi? ____________________

Name______________________________ Date______________________________

16. What were some of the important Renaissance and Baroque forms of instrumental music? ______________________________

17. Who were J.S. Bach and George Frideric Handel? ______________________________

18. What was the War of the Buffoons? ______________________________

19. Who was Mozart? ______________________________

20. What physical trauma did Beethoven have to endure? ______________________________

21. Why could Franz Liszt have been called a piano "terminator"? ______________________________

22. Who was Richard Wagner? ______________________________

23. What's the difference between Impressionism and Expressionism? ______________________________

24. What important form of composition did Schönberg develop? ______________________________

25. Who were some of the important people in the history of jazz? ______________________________

26. Why did rock and roll music become so popular so quickly? ______________________________

# ANSWER KEYS

**Music in the Middle Ages Question Countdown (page 2)**

1. A.D. 450 and 1450
2. Christianity
3. Romanesque
4. cathedrals or monasteries
5. nobility, clergy, and peasantry
6. toward the end
7. liturgical singing
8. vocal music
9. instruments
10. organ

**Crossword Puzzle (page 3)**

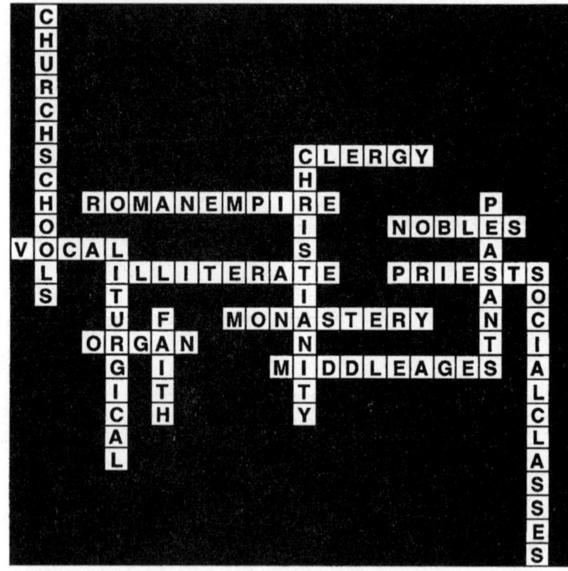

**Pope Gregory I and the Dove (page 5)**

1. the Scriptures
2. feasts and celebrations
3. Greek, Hebrew, and Syrian music
4. Roman Catholic Church
5. 14 years
6. a dove
7. so chants could be taken to churches throughout Europe
8. the Spirit of God

**Leonin and Perotin Go to School Question Countdown (page 7)**

1. polyphony
2. the development of precise notation of music
3. Leonin
4. Notre Dame Cathedral
5. organum
6. Perotin
7. three and four parts
8. motet
9. sacred or secular
10. sacred: religious theme; secular: nonreligious theme

**Word Search (page 8)**

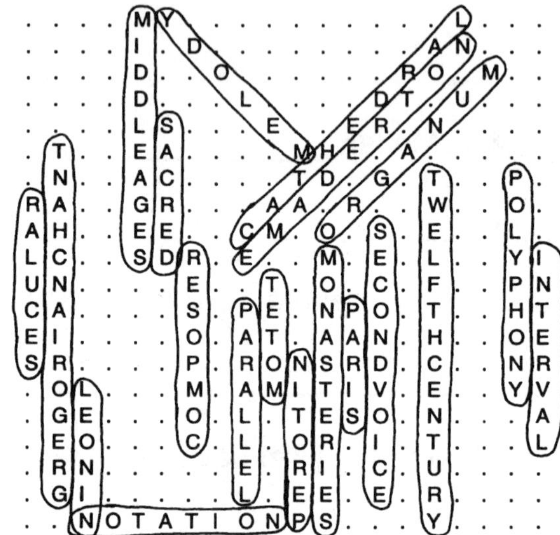

**Troubadours, Trouvères, and Jongleurs (page 10)**

1. finder or inventor
2. secular music
3. the Roman Catholic church
4. jongleurs
5. secular music
6. strengthened their spirits
7. played instruments, sang and danced, juggled, showed tricks
8. traveling newspaper
9. as vagabonds
10. love songs, political and moral tunes, war songs, laments, and dance songs

**"New Art" vs. "Old Art" (page 12)**

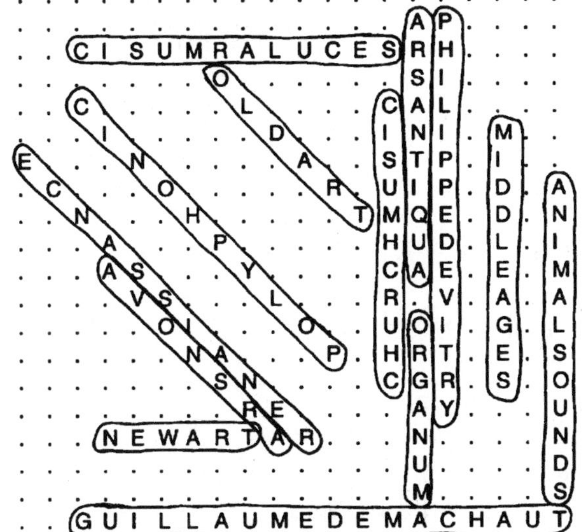

**Sacred Music: The Motet and Mass (page 18)**

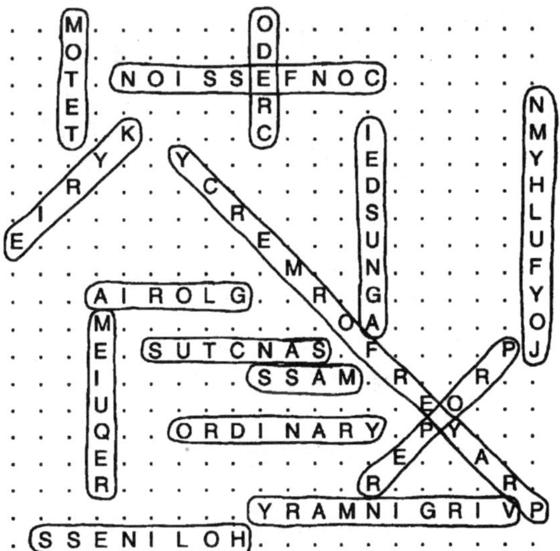

**Music in the Renaissance (page 14)**

1. rebirth
2. a time of creativity, exploration, and adventure
3. the arts, the sciences, and learning
4. Martin Luther
5. the middle and upper classes
6. the printing press and movable type
7. every educated person
8. from churches to courts of the nobility
9. instrumental forms
10. allowed compositions to be printed, duplicated, and sent throughout Europe

**Josquin: The Man, the Myth, the Great (page 16)**

1. Josquin des Prez
2. Martin Luther
3. the pitting of one melody against another
4. unusual ease in the use of counterpoint and depth of emotion
5. He composed a tremendous amount of music.
6. the motet
7. explore the newly developing compositional techniques of the Renaissance
8. motets and mass settings
9. He helped to close the Medieval period and open the Renaissance.
10. Medieval and Renaissance

**Secular Music: Renaissance "Pop" (page 20)**

1. our "pop" music
2. chanson, madrigal, and instrumental dance music
3. three voices
4. Johannes Ockeghem and Roland de Lassus
5. love poetry of the French Renaissance
6. instrumental dance music
7. whether the dance was indoors or outdoors
8. shawm and sackbutt
9. pavane, saltarello, galliard, allemande, and the ronde
10. the madrigal

**Palestrina and Gabrieli: The Italians are Coming (page 22)**

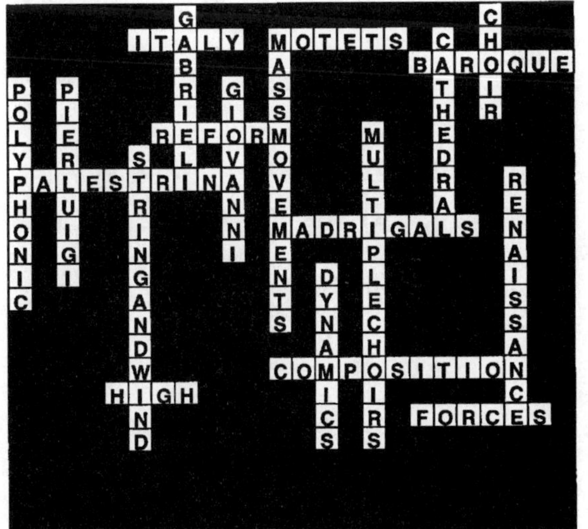

**Music in the Baroque Period**
**Question Countdown (page 24)**

1. Handel, Bach, Vivaldi, or Monteverdi
2. a commissioned work
3. the aristocracy, churches, opera houses, and municipalities
4. one main melody accompanied by other voices or instruments
5. solo singers vs. chorus or voices vs. instruments
6. unity of mood
7. rhythmic patterns at the beginning of a piece repeated throughout
8. opening melody heard throughout the course of a piece of music
9. sudden shifts in dynamics
10. the orchestra and opera

**Crossword Puzzle (page 25)**

**Claudio Monteverdi: Opera is Cool! (page 27)**

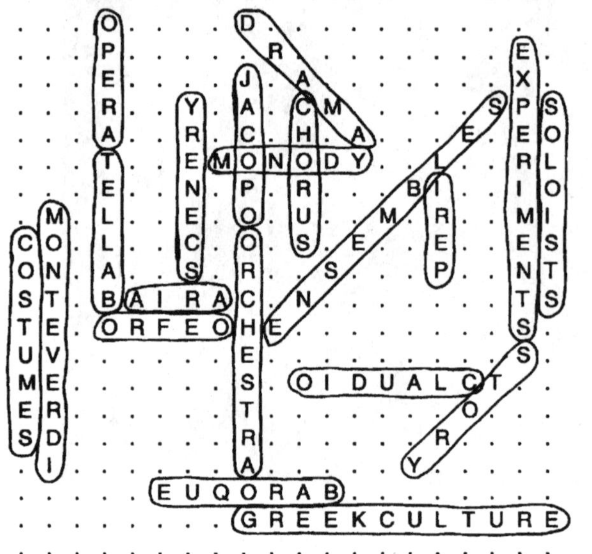

**Instruments Can Make Beautiful Music, Too! (page 29)**

| | | |
|---|---|---|
| 1. o | 6. c | 11. f |
| 2. j | 7. m | 12. e |
| 3. l | 8. n | 13. g |
| 4. a | 9. k | 14. b |
| 5. h | 10. d | 15. i |

**Bach and Handel: Putting it Together (page 31)**

1. Johann Sebastian Bach and George Frideric Handel
2. Eisenach, Germany
3. virtuoso
4. cantata
5. an opera is dramatized
6. Halle, Germany
7. a large-scale musical work for solo voices and orchestra based on a story from the Bible
8. church or concert hall
9. *Messiah*
10. twelve

**Music in the Classical Period (page 33)**

1. jazz, rock, or popular styles
2. eighteenth and nineteenth centuries
3. art history
4. stressing balance and clarity of structure
5. not limited by boundaries of countries, cities, or classes
6. the aristocracy and the middle class
7. Franz Joseph Haydn, Wolfgang Amadeus Mozart, and Ludwig van Beethoven
8. free from the service of an aristocratic family
9. Beethoven
10. Mozart

**The War of the Buffoons (page 35)**

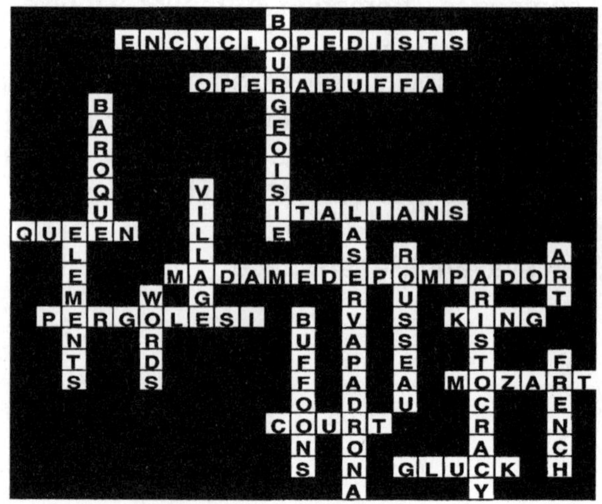

**Franz Joseph Haydn and the Esterhazys (page 37)**
1. Rohrau, Austria
2. No, he was a wheelwright.
3. St. Stephen's Cathedral in Vienna
4. His voice changed.
5. teaching, accompanying, and performing with roving musicians
6. He incorporated folk tunes in his compositions.
7. Esterhazy
8. the best in Europe
9. the death of the prince
10. England

**Amadeus—A Child Prodigy Question Countdown (page 39)**
1. Salzburg, Austria
2. Leopold Mozart; He was a composer and violinist in the court of the Archbishop of Salzburg.
3. age 5
4. sonatas, concertos, symphonies, religious works, operas
5. as a freelance musician
6. Emperor Joseph II
7. He married Constance Weber.
8. He couldn't get financial aid from his father.
9. his attitude and lack of decorum
10. He was penniless and not well known or highly acclaimed.

**Word Unscramble (page 40)**
1. operas
2. patronage system
3. freelance
4. empress
5. Leopold Mozart
6. Paris
7. Wolfgang Mozart
8. Emperor Joseph
9. composer
10. child prodigy
11. Munich
12. Salzburg
13. aristocracy
14. Mozart's father
15. Vienna
16. symphonies
17. appointment
18. Constance Weber
19. London
20. mastery

**Ludwig Van Beethoven: A Stormy Life (page 42)**
1. Ludwig van Beethoven
2. the Rhineland
3. They were singers at the court of the local prince.
4. assistant organist in the court chapel
5. harpsichordist in the court orchestra
6. Mozart
7. because of Beethoven's volcanic temperament and free spirit
8. the greatly increased amount of music publishing
9. He became deaf.
10. as a standard of excellence for their own compositions

**Music in the Romantic Period (page 44)**

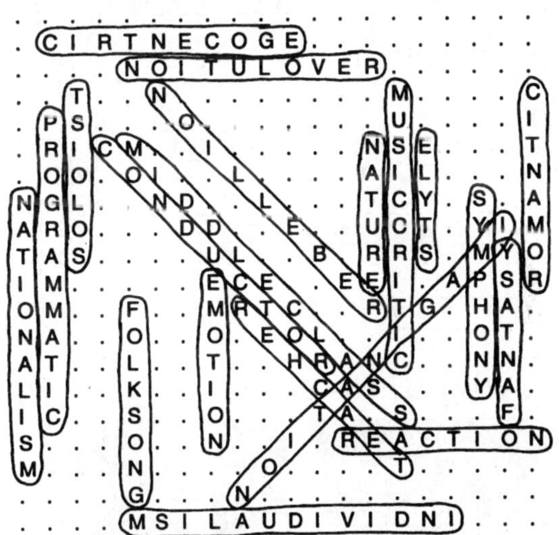

**Schubert's Unfinished Symphony (page 46)**
1. Franz Peter Schubert
2. the violin
3. his first symphony
4. 1,000
5. Romantic symphony
6. *The Unfinished Symphony*
7. three or four movements
8. 31
9. to be buried near Beethoven
10. nine symphonies

**Franz Liszt: The Piano Terminator (page 48)**
1. Hungary
2. Schubert and Beethoven
3. Paris, France
4. Paganini
5. 8 to 12 hours a day
6. Pianos weren't very sturdy, and Liszt was a physically strong player.
7. conduct
8. the works of his contemporaries, such as Berlioz, Schumann, and Wagner
9. music criticism and writing books
10. They were unappreciated and not well received.

**Romantic Opera: Bigger Must Be Better (page 50)**

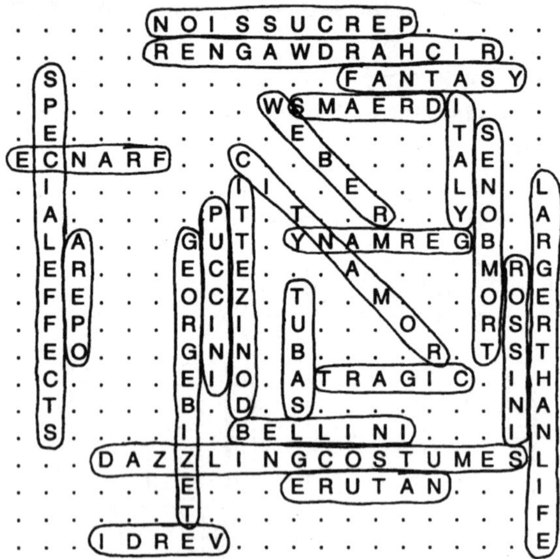

**Richard Wagner: The Egocentric (page 52)**

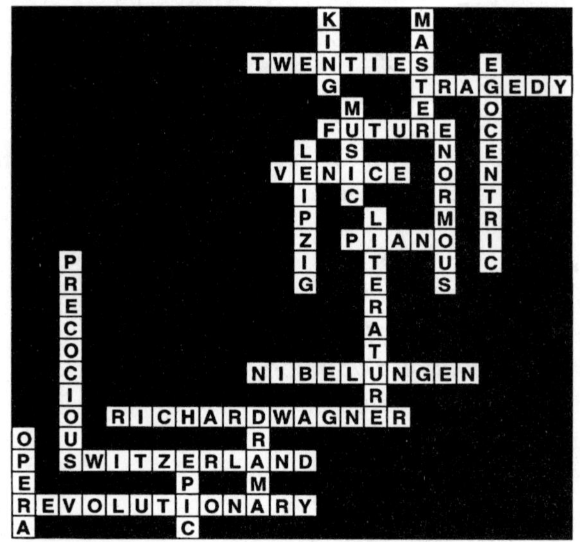

**Impressionism and Expressionism (page 54)**
1. an impression or a footprint
2. Claude Monet and August Renoir
3. with short strokes or flecks of colored patches
4. Claude Debussy
5. "Reflections in the Water," "Clouds," and "Sounds and Perfumes Swirl in the Evening Air"
6. creating a certain mood or atmosphere
7. Germany
8. Arnold Schönberg, Alban Berg, Anton von Webern
9. distort something so as to shock the audience
10. They sought to express the inner turmoil.

**Music in the Twentieth Century (page 56)**
1. dawning
2. developments
3. synthesizer
4. variety of styles
5. traditional
6. new sounds
7. abandonment
8. popular music
9. modern rock
10. technological
11. twentieth century
12. new age
13. electronic music
14. jazz
15. atonal music
16. twelve tones
17. composition
18. harmony
19. additional styles

**Schönberg and Atonality (page 58)**

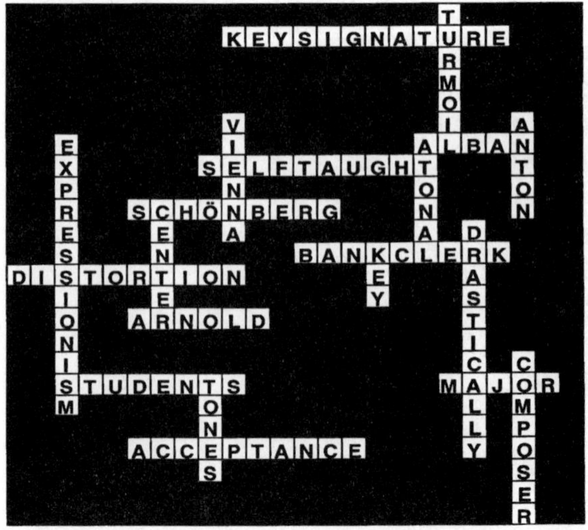

**The Jazz Scene**
**Question Countdown (page 60)**

1. jazz
2. Scott Joplin
3. "Maple Leaf Rag" and "The Entertainer"
4. African-Americans
5. piano, string bass, drummer, banjo, and guitar
6. cornet, trumpet, saxophone, piano, clarinet, and trombone
7. New Orleans
8. Chicago
9. Count Basie, Glenn Miller, Tommy Dorsey, Duke Ellington, and Benny Goodman
10. improvisation and spontaneous performance

**Word Search (page 61)**

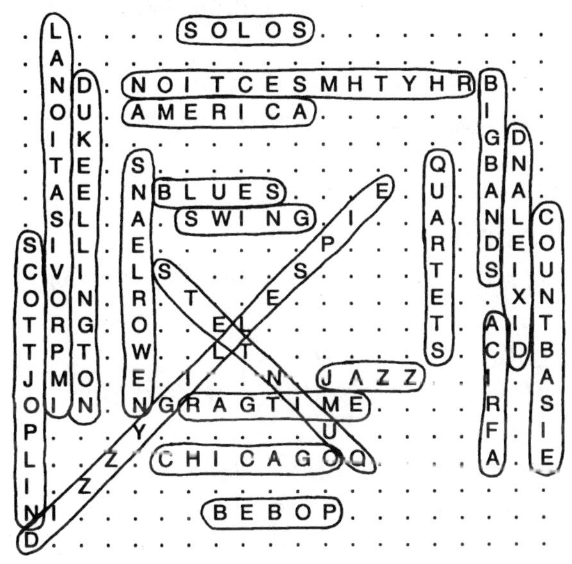

**Rock and Roll and Beyond (page 63)**

1. America
2. rhythm and blues, jazz, and country-western music
3. Bill Hayley and His Comets
4. Elvis Presley
5. It was a form of rebellion.
6. The Beatles
7. from the emphasis these tunes placed on gospel origins and heartfelt words
8. musicals, pieces for choirs, church music, and symphonies
9. It took elements of music from the past and combined them in new and different ways.
10. Europe

**Review Questions (pages 64-65)**

Answers may vary. Teachers should accept anwers supported by information in the narrative pages.

# BIBLIOGRAPHY

## General Reading

Abraham, Gerald. *The Concise Oxford History of Music.* New York: Oxford University Press, 1979.

Borroff, Edith. *Music in Europe and the United States.* Englewood Cliffs, New Jersey: Prentice-Hall Inc., 1990.

Cannon, Beekman C., Alvin H. Johnson, and William C. Waite. *The Art of Music.* New York: Crowell, 1960.

Crocker, Richard L. *A History of Musical Style.* New York: Dover, 1986.

Grout, Donald Jay, and Claude Palisca. *A History of Western Music.* 4th ed. New York: W.W. Norton, 1988.

Lang, Paul Henry, ed. *Music in Western Civilization.* New York: W.W. Norton, 1941.

Rosenstiel, Leonie, ed. *Schirmer History of Music.* New York: Schirmer Books, 1982.

Sachs, Curt. *Rise of Music in the Ancient World, East and West.* New York: W.W. Norton, 1943.

Strunk, Oliver. *Source Readings in Music History.* New York: W.W. Norton, 1950.

Wold, Milo, et al. *An Introduction to Music and Art in the Western World.* 8th ed. Dubuque, Iowa: Wm. C. Brown Co., 1987.

## Basic References

Hitchcock, H. Wiley, and Stanley Sadie, ed. *The New Grove Dictionary of American Music.* 4 vols. London: Macmillan Press, 1986.

*New Oxford History of Music.* 10 vols. London: Oxford, 1954–1975.

Randel, Don, ed. *The New Harvard Dictionary of Music.* Cambridge: Harvard University Press, 1986.

Sadie, Stanley, ed. *New Grove Dictionary of Music.* 20 vols. London: Macmillan, 1980.*

Slonimsky, Nicholas. *Baker's Biographical Dictionary of Musicians.* 8th ed. New York: Shirmer Books, 1992.

Thompson, Oscar. *International Cyclopedia of Music and Musicians.* 10th ed. Edited by Oscar Thompson and Bruce Bohle. New York: W.W. Dodd, 1975.

**Authors note:* This edition of Grove is by far the most comprehensive in the English language. It contains extended articles on every facet of music as well as extensive biographical entries.

## Periods

### Middle Ages (450–1450)

Arnold, John. *Medieval Music.* New York: Oxford University Press, 1986.

Cattin, Giulio. *Music of the Middle Ages.* Translated by Steven Botterill. New York: Cambridge University Press, 1985.

Fenlon, Ian, ed. *Early Music History.* 7 vols. Cambridge, England: Cambridge University Press, 1981 and following.

Hoppin, Richard H. *Medieval Music.* Ch. I–VII. New York: W.W. Norton, 1978.

Hughes, Andrew. *Medieval Music: The Sixth Liberal Art,* 2nd ed. Toronto: University of Toronto Press, 1980.

Seay, Albert. *Music in the Medieval World,* 2nd ed. Englewood Cliffs: Prentice-Hall, 1975.

**Renaissance (1450–1600)**

Bukofzer, Manfred. *Studies in Medieval and Renaissance Music.* New York: W.W. Norton, 1950.

Carpenter, Nan Cooke. *Music in the Medieval and Renaissance Universities.* Norman, Oklahoma: University of Oklahoma Press, 1958.

Jeppeson, Knud. *The Style of Palestrina and the Dissonance.* London: Oxford, 1927.

Reese, Gustav. Edited by Stanley Sadie. *New Grove High Renaissance Masters.* New York: W.W. Norton, 1984.

Walker, Ernest. *A History of Music in England.* London: Oxford, 1952.

**Baroque (1600–1750)**

Bianconi, Lorenzo. *Music in the Seventeenth Century.* Translated by David Bryant. New York: Cambridge University Press, 1987.

Flower, Newman. *Handel.* London: Cassell and Co., 1959.

Geiringer, Karl. *The Bach Family.* New York: Oxford, 1954.

Gleason, Harold, and Warren Becker. *Music in the Baroque,* 3rd ed. Van Nuys, California: Alfred Publishing Co., 1979.

Grout, Donald J. *A Short History of Opera,* 3rd ed. New York: Columbia University Press, 1973.

Palisca, Claude V. *Baroque Music.* Englewood Cliffs, New Jersey: Prentice-Hall, 1968.

**Classical (1750–1820)**

Burney, Dr. Charles. *An Eighteenth Century Musical Tour in Central Europe and the Netherlands.* New York: Oxford, 1959.

Carse, Adam. *The Orchestra in the Eighteenth Century.* Cambridge, England: W. Hetter, 1940.

Dent, E.J. *Mozart's Operas,* 2nd ed. New York: Oxford, 1991.

Einstein, Alfred. *Mozart: His Character and Work.* New York: Oxford, 1945.

Geiringer, Karl. *Haydn, A Creative Life in Music.* New York: W.W. Norton, 1946.

Pastelli, Giorgio. *Age of Mozart and Beethoven.* Translated by Eric Cross. New York: Cambridge University Press, 1984.

Pauly, Reinhard G. *Music in the Classic Period,* 2nd ed. Englewood Cliffs, New Jersey: Prentice-Hall, 1973.

Rosen, Charles. *The Classical Style.* New York: Viking, 1971.

**Romantic (1820–1900)**

Abraham, Gerald. *A Hundred Years of Music.* New York: Knopf, 1938.

Barzun, Jacques. *Berlioz and the Romantic Century,* 2 vols. New York: Little, Brown, 1950.

Chase, Gilbert. *America's Music.* New York: McGraw-Hill, 1955.

Donnington, Robert. *The Opera.* New York: Harcourt, Brace, Jovanovich, 1978.

Kramer, Lawrence. *Music and Poetry: The Nineteenth Century and After.* Berkeley: University of California Press, 1984.

Longyear, Rey M. *Nineteenth-Century Romanticism in Music,* 3rd ed. Englewood Cliffs, New Jersey: Prentice-Hall, 1988.
Newman, Ernest. *The Wagner Operas.* New York: Knopf, 1949.
Plantinga, Leon. *Romantic Music.* New York: W.W. Norton, 1984.
Soloman, Maynard. *Beethoven.* New York: Schirmer, 1977.
Thayer, A.W. *Life of Ludwig van Beethoven.* Princeton, New Jersey: Princeton University Press, 1964.

**Twentieth Century**

Berendt, Joachim. *The Jazz Book.* Westport, Connecticut: Lawrence Hill, 1975.
Brown, Charles T. *The Art of Rock and Roll,* 2nd ed. New York: Prentice-Hall, 1987.
Carlson, Effie B. *Bio-Bibliographical Dictionary of Twelve Tone and Serial Composers.* Ann Arbor, Michigan: UMI, no date.
Cope, David. *New Directions in Music.* Dubuque, Iowa: Wm. C. Brown Company Publishers, 1984.
Dorter, Tom, and Greg Arbruster. *The Art of Electronic Music.* New York: Morrow, 1985.
Eimert, Herbert, and Karlheinz Stockhausen. *Anton Webern.* Valley Forge, Pennsylvania: European-American Press, 1958.
Ernst, David. *The Evolution of Electronic Music.* New York: G. Schirmer, 1987.
Ewen, David. *All the Years of American Popular Music.* Englewood Cliffs, New Jersey: Prentice-Hall, 1977.
Gammond, Peter. *The Oxford Companion to Popular Music.* New York: Oxford University Press, 1991.
Hintoff, Nat. *Jazz Is.* New York: Limelight Editions, 1984.
Hodier, André. *Jazz, Its Evolution and Essence.* New York: Grove Press, 1986.
Kaufman, Fredreck, and John P. Guckin. *The African Roots of Jazz.* Van Nuys, Claifornia: Alfred Publishing Co., 1979.
Leibowitz, René. *Schoenberg and His School.* New York: Philosophical Library, 1949.
Marcus, Greil. *The Aesthetics of Rock.* Jersey City, New Jersey: Da Capo, 1987.
Martin, William R., and Julius Drossing. *Music of the 20th Century.* Englewood Cliffs, New Jersey: Prentice-Hall, 1980.
Morgan, Robert. *Twentieth Century Music.* New York: W.W. Norton, 1991.
Pleasants, Henry. *The Agony of Modern Music.* New York: Simon and Schuster, 1955.
Salzman, Eric. *Twentieth-Century Music: An Introduction,* 2nd ed. Englewood Cliffs, New Jersey: Prentice-Hall, 1974.
Schuller, Gunther. *Early Jazz: Its Roots and Musical Development.* New York: Oxford, 1968.
Sessions, Roger. *The Musical Experience of the Composer, Performer, Listener.* Princeton, New Jersey: Princeton University Press, 1950.
Stuckenschmidt, H.H. *Twentieth Century Music.* Translated By Richard Deveson. New York: McGraw Hill, 1969.
Whitcomb, Ian. *After the Ball: Pop Music from Rag to Rock,* Rev. ed. New York: Limelight Ed., 1986.
Wilder, Alec. *American Popular Song: The Great Innovators, 1900–1950.* New York: Oxford, 1972.
Williams, Martin, ed. *The Art of Jazz: Ragtime to Bebop.* Jersey City, New Jersey: Da Capo, 1981.